CRUCIFYING AMERICA

CRUCIFYING AMERICA

THE UNHOLY ALLIANCE BETWEEN THE CHRISTIAN RIGHT AND WALL STREET

CJ WERLEMAN

dangerous™ little books

First Published in Great Britain 2013
by Dangerous Little Books

Cover illustration by Daniel Espinal (http://chokosup.wordpress.com)

Senator Elisabeth Warren (D-Ma)

She gets it!

Images of small men usually
arise and persist widely only because
big men find good use for them.

C. WRIGHT MILLS, *WHITE COLLAR*

CJ Werleman is the author of *God Hates You. Hate Him Back; Jesus Lied He Was Only Human;* and *Koran Curious*. A columnist for *The Contributor*, and a regular guest on a number of radio talk shows, including the Sirius network, CJ is also a keynote speaker at major secular events. Learn more at www.cjwerleman.com.

Also by CJ Werleman

God Hates You. Hate Him Back

Jesus Lied. He Was Only Human

Koran Curious

PRAISE

"With the passion and urgency the subject deserves, 'Crucifying America' is an unabashed wake-up call to a nation that has allowed religious conservatives to hijack public policy."

David Niose, author of 'Nonbeliever Nation: The Rise of Secular Americans'

"'Crucifying America' is an effective surgical strike on the runaway theocrats and their well-financed assault on the American political system. Powerful stuff."

Seth Andrews, author of 'Deconverted: A Journey From Religion to Reason'

"There's no sacred cow nor bullshit CJ doesn't eviscerate with his keystrokes. He's the voice of the next generation of atheists. God help us."

Tina Dupuy (Syndicated Columnist)

"In 'Crucifying America', Werleman makes a compelling case for how the 'unholy alliance' between the Christian Right and corporate America has negatively impacted economic and social policy."

David G. McAfee, author of 'Mom, Dad, I'm an Atheist'

"CJ Werleman makes the compelling case that the supposed wall between church and state has been slowly chipped away and eroded, and now looks like more of a communion wafer – looks pretty, but doesn't even slightly do what it claims. If you don't love this book, you're in the demographic that should really be reading this book."

Jake Farr-Wharton, author of 'Letters To Christian Leaders: Hollow Be Thy Claims'

CONTENTS

plu·toc·ra·cy

1. governance by wealthy: the rule of a society by its wealthiest people

2. society ruled by wealthy: a society that is ruled by its wealthiest members

3. wealthy ruling class: a wealthy social class that controls or greatly influences the government of a society

the·oc·ra·cy

1. government by god: government by a god or by priests

2. community governed by god: a community governed by a god or priests

FOREWORD

I will start this book with a simple statement: a statement that will place the message of this book into some kind of overall context; a statement that should remind any secularist or humanist of what is at stake in this country, at least politically, in the next several cycles of local, state, and federal elections. That statement is this:

The South has never gotten over losing the Civil War.

End statement.

Given the Civil War's battlefield hostilities ended some 150 years ago, it's unlikely the South will get over it anytime soon. Michael Lind, Whitehead Senior Fellow at the New America Foundation, put the above statement into some present day context when he wrote in a 2009 *Daily Beast* article:

> The battle in Washington is not between liberals and conservatives; it is between the Union and the South. The rest of the country needs to understand... this [Republican Party] is the party whose spiritual ancestors are the old Southern conservative Democrats, like John. C. Calhoun and Jefferson Davis and Strom Thurmond and Orval Faubus.

From the conception of the Constitution, the South opposed what they saw as too much control awarded to the Federal government, and too little sovereignty bestowed upon the states. Inevitably, arguments arose over taxation, domestic policy, the role of the military, and of course slavery.

i

When Illinois born Abraham Lincoln defeated the Kentucky good ole boy John C. Breckinridge in the 1860 election, the South did what Rick Perry's Texas, among other bumfuck states, threatens today: they seceded from the Union and formed their own little haven of ass backwards, Baptist Christianity-fueled hate monkey oppression.

The Confederacy loved its 19th century version of 1980s apartheid South Africa so much that they felt compelled by God to impose it on their far more enlightened neighbors in the North. So, at exactly 4:30am on the morning of Friday April 12, 1861 the Confederate Army fired the first shot of the Civil War. Not merely a volley of shots, as much as 34 straight hours of artillery bombardment on the Union-manned Fort Sumter, a mile or so from the shores of the most politically retarded state in the country, South Carolina. The Confederates won this battle but, like in the case of Japan attacking Pearl Harbor, the militarily weaker South had awoken a sleeping giant. In fact, many have amusingly likened the South's commencement of the Civil War to the madness of Poland invading Germany in 1939.

Obviously, we all know how the story ends. The South loses the war, but not until 600,000 Americans are needlessly slaughtered on home soil. The South's defeat, though, is unlike that of any other foe the nation has defeated abroad. You see, when one travels throughout Japan one does not find statues honoring Tojo or Kanin. In Germany, one does not find monuments built in honor of Nazi storm troopers. But in the South there are all kinds of Civil War obelisks, dedications, and monuments or, as I like to call them, second place trophies honoring all kinds of nefarious slave-loving generals and out of the closet Klansmen, among other notable white supremacists. Nine states still celebrate Confederate Memorial Day (Alabama, Florida, North Carolina, Georgia, South Carolina, Tennessee, Louisiana, Mississippi, and Texas).

In the small town of Abbeville, South Carolina, is a granite obelisk that honors the memory of the Confederate soldier. On it is the inscription: "The world shall yet decide, in truth's clear far-off light, that the soldiers who wore the gray and died with Lee were right."

Take a moment to think about that. "The soldiers who wore the gray and died with Lee were right." That the cause of the Confederacy – a dissolution of the United States so that the South may preserve the commercial interests of slavery – was a noble, righteous and just cause. The first time I heard of this monument I dismissed it as something that presumably was erected in honor of the fallen during the sorrow of the battle. Nay, it was erected in 1906, and then replaced with a new and improved obelisk with the same wording in 1996. It's still there today.

Despite political feel good rhetoric, there are two Americas. Not just ideologically, but geographically. That's what still makes this country unique among other Western democracies. America is two distinct nations with a distinguishable border that runs the entire breadth of the country from the Mason-Dixon line across the southern border of Pennsylvania, finishing in some Baptist church somewhere in rural Texas.

The most concise book on the topic of Civil War era dynamics in the modern political landscape is Chuck Thompson's *Better Off Without 'Em: A Northern Manifesto for Southern Secession*. This won't be the last time I refer to Thompson's work in this book, but on the issue of explaining the current political divide, he writes:

The unified southern resistance to every initiative from any "liberal" administration has deep historic roots. The persistent defiance of every Democratic attempt to deal intelligently with national problems – be they recession, debt, or childhood obesity – has nothing to with political ideology, taxes, health care, or acceptable degrees of federal authority. It has everything to do with nullification, disruption, zealotry, and division. It's part of a time-sharpened effort to debilitate nearly every northern-led government by injecting it with the Seven Deadly Sins of Southern Politics: demagogic dishonesty, religious fanaticism, willful obstructionism, disregard for own self-interest, corporate supplication, disproportionate influence, and military adventurism.

Now, let's not forget that the entire South was reliably Democratic until President Lyndon Johnson signed into law the Civil Rights Act of 1964. At the time of the Act's passage, LBJ said, "We (Democrats) have lost the South for a generation." It's now almost two generations later, so where are we now? In the 2004 election, John Kerry, a Democratic northerner from Massachusetts, failed to win a single state in the South. In 2008 and 2012, Obama carried more or less a mere 10 percent of the white vote on the way to winning the presidency twice. So, it's not just the Civil War the South hasn't gotten over, it's also the Civil Rights Act. Imagine how long it is going to take before they accept Obamacare, much less a gay married couple from San Francisco having sex on a Confederate flag.

Nothing separates the North from the South like white pride and religion. A recent University of Rochester study suggests that the legacy of slavery is what leads white people to turn Republican in the South, even today:

> Drawing on a sample of more than 39,000 southern whites, we show that whites who currently live in counties that had high concentrations of slaves in 1860 are on average more conservative and express colder feelings towards African Americans than whites who live elsewhere in the South. That is, the larger the number of slaves in his or her county of residence in 1860, the greater the probability that a white Southerner today will identify as a Republican, express opposition to race-coded policies such as affirmative action, and express greater racial resentment towards African Americans.

The South is fixated on everything related to controlling race, sex, religious practice, abortion laws, and repealing every progressive law that has come out of the federal government. Their worldview, in which nuance is absent, sees only good and evil in terms of what was written in the Bible 4,000 years ago by a tribe of Middle Eastern goat shepherds. To compromise with someone who doesn't accept the Bible literally is to literally compromise with a Satanic force, in their eyes, and to do so would only guarantee God sends another tornado hurtling towards the good Christian people of Oklahoma as punishment. It's funny (not haha funny) how God rarely sends natural disasters careening into the far less religious North.

More concerning is the fact that the South never has and never will accept the separation of Church and State. It's just not in their DNA make-up, and is incongruent with their simple minded biblical worldview. In fact, it's the public goal of the South and the Christian Right to abolish the theocratic firewall so as they may turn America into a Christian theocracy. Hyperbole? No! Facts? Well, the Texas Republican Party Platform is this: "Our Party pledges to do everything within its power to dispel the myth of separation of Church and State." Christian Coalition founder Pat Robertson describes the church-state separation as "a lie" and "a distortion foisted on us over the past few years by left-wingers." Senator James Inhofe (R-Oklahoma) called it "the phoniest argument there is." A George W. Bush appointee to the 11th circuit court of appeals declared that the First Amendment does not mandate "a strict separation of church and state." Former and disgraced Republican House Majority Leader Tom DeLay said, "Standing up and rebuking this notion of separation of church and state that has been imposed upon us over the last 40 or 50 years. You see, I don't believe there is a separation of church and state." I can go on and on and on, but even the most rudimentary Google search reveals a treasure trove of Christian fundamentalist and right wing history revisionist absurdity. But to leave you in no doubt that the rot travels all the way to the highest judicial branch of government, Supreme Court Justice Scalia said, at an event called Religious Freedom Day, that the separation of Church and State would come under scrutiny under a Supreme Court with a Scalia majority.

League of the South founder Michael Hill said in a recent interview, "The South still reveres the tenets of our historic Christian faith. Our primary allegiance is to the Lord Jesus Christ and His Holy Church. Southerners are the second most populous stateless nation included in the encyclopedia, after the Tamils of southern India. The thirteen-state South remains the twelfth in population of all nation states of the earth." In other words, they want to take over the North and turn the entire country into their idea of Christian Reconstructionism, which is a political movement to convert the United States into a theocracy in which dissenters, adulterers, homosexuals, bisexuals, transgenders, infidels and atheists would be incarcerated or exterminated.

The Republican Party is not only the party of the corporate eite, it's also the party of the South. The party's leaders are predominantly Southern. Senate Minority Leader Mitch McConnell is from Kentucky. House Speaker John Boehner is from Cincinnati, Ohio, but Cincinnati is as close to the South as a northern city can be given the city's airport is actually in Kentucky. House Majority Leader Eric Cantor is from Virginia. And then there are the likely 2016 presidential hopefuls. With the exception of New Jersey Governor Chris Christie, and the pathologically homophobic Rick Santorum, the rest of the clown car are as southern as Colonel Sanders. Bigots make the most delicious chicken. Rand Paul is from Kentucky. Bobby Jindal is from Louisiana. Mitch Daniels is from Oklahoma. Jeb Bush is from Florida via Texas. Marco Rubio is from Florida. Rick Perry is from Texas. Yes, for all intents and purposes, I include Texas as a state of the South. Banning tampons from the State House, and inserting Creationism into school textbooks earns the Lone Star State that honor.

Thompson writes:

> The Solid South's evangelical rigidity of thought not only confers upon the region an inordinate influence in presidential politics, it enables the

South to assume a disproportionate control of Congress through assumption of congressional committee chairmanships. The seniority system for chairmanships adopted by Congress in 1910 has allowed change-fearing southern voters – who tend more than others to return the same officials to Washington year in year out – to seize control of House and Senate leadership positions. Thus have the most reactionary and entrenched politicians in the country wrested control of the laws and policies of the entire nation.

With the Christian Right's goal to turn the secular North into the religious South, corporations are all too happy to turn the unionized North into the de-unionized South. In fact, the South is a captive tool of corporate ideology. It has been this way since the South embraced the pro-corporate Republican Party in the hours after a Democrat President dared to give black people equal rights in 1964. As a result, the mostly poor working class South has seen corporate taxes lowered, its schools defunded and its unions obliterated. And yet they still adore the Republican Party. Talk about beaten wife syndrome. Effectively, the South has become the North's Mexico. Or better still, we should rename the South, North Mexico. Lind wrote in *The Daily Beast*, "Unable to compete on the basis of public investment and public education, the South of the 21st century, like a broken-down banana republic, now uses anti-union laws and low taxes to lure corporate investment from the rest of the country."

In just one example, average wages for autoworkers in the South are 20 to 30 percent lower than in Michigan.

Thus, auto manufacturers have been leaving the North en-masse to take advantage of cheap non-union-protected labor. Thompson says:

> The South is bad for the American economy in the same way that China and Mexico are bad for the American economy. By keeping corporate tax rates low, public schools underfunded, and workers' right to organize negligible, it's southern politicians who make it so. By separating itself [secession] from this suppurating cancer in our midst, the rest of the country would at least be able to deal with the South as it would any other Third World entity, rather than as the in-house parasite that bleeds the country far more than it contributes to its collective health.

That's strong rhetoric. I like strong rhetoric! Alarmingly, the rest of the country is being dragged by the cojones into adopting a Third World business model because the rest of the country is being undercut by a Third World economy that resides within the borders of the continental United States – the South.

For now, the North's firewall against becoming a full-blown corporate-driven theocratic banana republic, like that of the South, is the fact that corporations are unable to vote. But what if corporations partnered with the most politically agitated segment of the Republican Party, the Christian Right, to take control of local, state and federal governments with Republican, Jesus-approved candidates?

What then? Well, it's happening now. And this is what this book is about.

INTRODUCTION

There's something to be said for the theory of safety in numbers. As someone who grew up on the east coast of Australia, I was taught early the importance of surfing always with a friend. Mathematical probability has it that in the event of a shark attack the mere presence of my friend halves the likelihood of me becoming the "man in the grey suit's" dinner. Equally, no one wants to be the only Israeli on an airline hijacked by Islamic terrorists, nor does one wish to be the only gay Muslim at a Republican National Convention. For atheists, the safety in numbers principle is particularly pertinent because atheists remain the most disliked minority in America. The high distrust of atheists in this country stems from the fact that within the reliably red states of the country, for example, so few people actually come into physical contact with out of the closest non-believers in their day-to-day lives. For many, atheists remain strange and unfamiliar, which only heightens prejudicial mistrust. Thus, a great part of the atheist movement is concerned with educating the public that atheists are as moral and trustworthy as any other segment of society, if not more so, given the social data we have available. A study published in the online journal *Evolutionary Psychology* (July 2009) found that countries with the lowest rates of social dysfunction – based on more than 20 indicators, including rates for poverty, unemployment, crime and sexually transmitted disease – are the most secular or anti-religious. On the flip side, three of the five most dangerous cities in the U.S. are in the most pious state of Texas. The twelve states with the highest rate of burglary are reliably

1

religiously conservative. Twenty-four of the twenty-nine states with the highest rates of theft are reliably religiously conservative. Of the twenty-two states with highest rates of murder, seventeen are staunchly religiously conservative.

Unfortunately, a public library full of facts and an online scientific journal are hardly where one finds mouth-breathing flat earthers to wax lyrical. There's Christian-Mingle.com for that. Thus, underscoring the important role that atheist groups, of which there are now more than 2,000 in America today, play in not only helping promote public awareness but also in encouraging atheists out of the closet. You know, the whole safety in numbers thing.

With that in mind, I have some heart-warming news that will make the godless scream "Hallelujah!", or whatever else atheists scream in moments of being on the receiving end of a blowjob. The good news I speak of comes courtesy of the intellectual war that atheists and free thinkers have so valiantly fought against religious institutions since the release of Darwin's *Origins of the Species*.

In simplicity, the good news is *we are winning*! Nay, we are on the way to a philosophical victory so comprehensive that within the next two generations, religion will be a faith of the minority few in the United States of America. Christianity, like the some 30,000+ religions before it, is well on its way to becoming another historical road kill on the highway of bad ideas.

Every piece of social data suggests that those who favor faith and superstition over fact-based evidence will become the minority of this country by or before the end of this century. In fact, the number of Americans who do not believe in a deity doubled in the last decade of the previous century according to both the census of 2004 and the

American Religious Identification Survey (ARIS) of 2008 – with religious non-belief in the U.S. rising from 8.2 percent in 1990 to 14.2 percent in 2001. In 2013, that number is now above 16 percent.

If current trends continue, the crossing point, whereby atheists will equal the number of Christians in this country, will be in the year 2062. If that gives you reason to celebrate, then consider this: by the year 2130, the percentage of Americans who identify themselves as Christians will equal less than 1 percent. RIP Christianity! Don't let the door hit you on the ass on the way out.

In fact, the fastest growing religious faith in the United States is the group collectively labeled "Nones," who spurn organized religion in favor of non-defined skepticism about faith. About two-thirds of Nones say they are former believers. This is hugely significant. The number of Americans who do not identify with any religion continues to skyrocket. One-fifth of the U.S. public – and a third of adults under 30 – are religiously unaffiliated today, the highest percentages ever in Pew Research Center polling. For all political and social purposes, Nones are tantamount to atheists. If you don't have a belief in a specific god, you're an atheist. It doesn't matter what you call yourself. Now, here's another thing to consider: when it comes to polls about religion: we lie. For some reason, the sight of a pollster with a clipboard who is asking questions about our religiosity leads many of us to give the answer we *think* we should instead of the truth. Remember, there are many atheists who keep their non-belief a secret from family, co-workers, and neighbors, for any number of reasons. The case of former congressman Barney Frank (D-Ma) exemplifies this phenomenon. While still in congress,

Frank was comfortable outing himself as a homosexual. But his life-long atheism was kept a secret until retiring his political career. Tina Dupuy, editor-in-chief for The Contributor, writes, "When it comes to self-reporting religious devotion Americans cannot be trusted. We under-estimate our calories, over-state our height, under-report our weight and when it comes to piety – we lie like a prayer rug." The point being there are far more of us non-believers than polling data gives us credit for. We are fast becoming the silent majority.

Atheist groups, associations, and networks have literally sprung up in every town and city in America. Million dollar social awareness campaigns have rolled across small towns and big cities throughout America. In major cities, you see billboards with messages like, "Are you Good Without God? Millions Are!" "Don't Believe in God? You Are Not Alone." Others say, "In the Beginning, Man Created God." These campaigns have helped coerce millions of Americans out of the theological closet. They have helped many in-private atheists step out of the shadows. The trend is very much that Americans raised in Christian households are shunning the religion of their parents for any number of reasons: the advancement of human understanding; greater access to information; the scandals of the Catholic Church; and the over zealousness of the Christian Right.

Political scientists Robert Putman and David Campbell, and authors of *American Grace*, argue that the Christian Right's politicization of faith in the 1990s turned younger, socially liberal Christians away from churches, even as conservatives became more zealous. "While the Republican base has become ever more committed to mixing religion and politics, the rest of the country has been moving in the opposite direction."

When you add all these things together, it leads you to a dramatic yet never mentioned dynamic: atheists are the fastest growing minority in the U.S. today. More significantly, we make for being one of the most powerful voting blocs in the country, at least potentially. We now have the required critical mass to shape elections, laws, and leaders. Safety in numbers is growing into power in numbers. In 10, 20, 50 years, the Christian Right will hold little to no sway over the nation's identity. From these facts, among others, we can boast that ideological victory is within sight.

Now for the bad news:

We are winning the wrong game!

We are losing the right game. We are winning the cultural war, but the Christian Right is winning in the race to control the levers of power. They hold the keys to our democracy, while we have clever bumper stickers, funny t-shirts, and books that deride virgin births and angry sky gods. The soldiers of God are playing a game that can only be described as Jedi Knight-ish. Meanwhile, we are being made to look juvenile, bellicose, and downright moronic. The Christian Right is ripping our arms off at the shoulder and then slapping us in the face with the soggy bits. It's embarrassing, and if this were a football game the scoreboard would read: Christian right –120 versus free thinkers – 3. Someone invoke the mercy rule! Also, I hate football metaphors.

You see, all around this great country, atheists are meeting in cafes, living rooms and Holiday Inn conference rooms to meet, share donuts and talk about how we can remove "In God We Trust" from the dollar bill; and how best we deal with removing "One nation under God" from the Pledge of Allegiance, in an attempt to reverse the sneaky-handed 1954 bill pushed through congress in 1954 by Christian zealot President Eisenhower. We protest home school conventions; any display of the Ten Commandments; and there are even atheist groups who file lawsuits every winter in their respective cities to ensure nothing but the secular "meaning" of Christmas is promoted.

Look, all these actions are fine with me but, let's be honest, they make us look like assholes. And frankly, if you're filing legal action to prevent others from declaring, "Merry Christmas", then you most definitely are an asshole!

What's worse is that atheists are wasting far too much intellectual and emotional energy on battles that lack real political gain or consequence. In other words, we're taking pot shots at an ideological enemy that's out of range and forward marching in another direction, and where they're dropping their ordinance is hurting us. Greatly!

While we are busy playing the role of the nation's police force for political correctness, they are gerrymandering voting districts to ensure they regain and maintain control of the levers of congressional and gubernatorial power. While we chant, "Keep the Bible out of the classroom", they are helping legislate voter ID laws that disenfranchise millions of black, Hispanic, and student voters. While we demand a removal of God from the Pledge of Allegiance, they are stacking the courts with their ideological judicial wingnuts. While we are correcting Christmas carolers with, "Happy Holidays", they are mobilizing to ensure money buys them judges, congressmen and governors, which not only protects the interests of big corporations at the expense of the little guy, but will also protect the interests of the Christian Right – namely, putting an end to the gay, secular, liberal agenda, and, in turn, setting gender and racial equality back 50 years.

Poll after poll shows that a majority of Americans favor liberal policies, but our courts and legislatures are increasingly becoming controlled and driven by the Christian Right. Their victories are having a far more reaching impact on our lives and our secular democratic values than our small-minded wins to remove the 10 Commandments from some hic town's courthouse.

The 2012 election was a rejection of the Ayn Rand, "Fuck you, I have mine" thinking that permeates the Republican base. Recall *that* moment during *the* 2012 GOP debates when the moderator asked the following hypothetical: "What should happen if a healthy 30-year-old man who can afford insurance chooses not to buy it and then becomes catastrophically ill and needs intensive care for six months?" In unison, the predominantly Tea Party (Christian Right) audience yelled, "*Let him die!*" Thankfully a majority of the American public spurned that callous thinking, as the national electorate went on to demonstrate that a majority of Americans see this country as a center-left country. Simply, we don't want to be a country that says there's legitimate rape and there's illegitimate rape. There's just rape! We don't want to be a country that rejects science and facts. We want our kids to accept what 99.9 percent of the scientific community agrees to when it comes to evolution. We want our kids to accept climate change as fact, then fight to do something about it, so as to preserve their kids' future. We don't want our politicians to hold prayer sessions as the main means for fighting poverty. We don't want our political leaders to believe poverty is caused by the individual's lack of religious faith. We don't want a country that demonizes the less fortunate. We want a country that judges a person by the content of their character, and not by the color of their skin. We want our laws to not only favor the interests of business but equally or more so favor our communities, our skies, our water, and our food. We want a representative democracy. We want "One nation, indivisible, with liberty and justice for all" – not all of one kind, but all. These are the ideals that a majority of Americans want in this great nation today.

Well, that's what we wanted, and that's kind of what we were getting, to some degree, until something really bad happened on January 21, 2010. A date of infamy! For that was the day the Supreme Court ruled in favor of the billionaire Koch brothers over the Federal Election Commission. In that ruling, the highest court in the land ruled that money equals free speech, and corporations equal people. That was the moment that whatever chance we had of righting the wrongs that have led to growing social inequalities in this country was lost. That was the moment that all but guarantees a continuation of the shrinking of the middle class. That was the moment that presented billionaires and the wealthiest corporations an opportunity to partner with the Christian Right, so that a new era of pro-business and anti-government policies could be enacted in this country.

The partnership between the super rich and religious crazies is truly a match made in heaven, for the most politically agitated group of voters in America today are the evangelicals. Throw some red meat to their holier than thou rationalizations and they won't care what big business does to this great nation. They care for only one thing – turning America into a theocratic regime. In other words, fascism with a religious face! And don't be fooled by the flag-waving and the obnoxious jingoism; social conservatives do not love America unconditionally. They love America subject to their political agenda being carried out. They pledge allegiance to the flag (the Western world's last surviving loyalty oath), but subject only to Americans electing a president they supported, and one they presume God supports, too. Thus the reason why all 2012 GOP presidential candidates, with the exception of Mitt Romney (the Mormon), were quick to proclaim that God had told him/her to run. That none of the God-chosen candidates went onto to win the nomination or the election suggests God has an amazing sense of humor. Of course, that is if don't count the whole Holocaust thing.

How do the mega rich benefit from a partnership with the Christian Right? The rich represent less than 1 percent of the country, so they need someone to elect their right wing politicians, and who better than the most agitated and mobilized voting bloc in all the land – social conservatives?

The agenda of the mega rich and Wall Street is not something that's only shared in secret boardrooms, yacht clubs, and Tommy Bahamas' summer line launch parties; it's hidden in plain sight. For big corporations want only a few things: elimination of government regulations; the destruction of unions, labor laws, social security, unemployment insurance, public education, Medicare, Obamacare and, of course, they want lower taxes. In short, they want to "shrink government until it's small enough to drown the bathtub," to borrow a quote from tax elimination activist Grover Norquist. For them, and despite the overwhelming evidence that refutes their self-serving economic policy fairytales, they want to be able to profit every step of our lives, from the cradle to the grave.

So, what does the Christian Right gain out of this marriage? Well, they are the unwitting pawns of big money. They're too adorably moronic to know they're being used as ballot box lever pullers. If you doubt that, next time you see a Tea Party rally, count how many lower-middle class people are carrying "Americans for Prosperity" printed placards. AFP is actually a Koch brother funded think tank whose goal is to take away the rights of the working class.

Since the Supreme Court's decision on free speech, we have witnessed an alarming number of laws and bills emerging from state legislatures and courts that run further to the right. Republican legislatures in Colorado, Missouri, Montana, and Oklahoma, for example, have introduced bills intended to reintroduce the unconstitutional teaching of creationism and religious dogma in public school classrooms. Alabama, North Dakota, Mississippi, and Tennessee are among the latest Republican controlled states to impose restrictions on women's access to abortion and contraception. In fact, in the first three months of 2013, Republicans have put forward 694 provisions related to reproductive health, with more than half involving abortion restrictions. In Virginia, the attorney general is calling for a law against sodomy, notwithstanding the fact that the definition of sodomy includes consensual oral and anal sex between a man and a woman. North Carolina is the perfect metaphor for how the Christian Right, alongside the funding from billionaires, is hijacking democracy in state after state. In the 2008 and 2012 elections, the split of votes went virtually 50-50 Republican/Democrat, with

Candidate Obama winning the state with a less than one percent margin over John McCain, and Romney winning the Tar Heel state by the same narrow margin over Obama in 2012. In simple terms, North Carolina is as purple as a state can be, but strangely, and for reasons we will go into depth on later, not only has a Republican governor but also a near two-thirds Republican majority in its elected assemblies. This has allowed this purple state to push ahead with one of the most radical right wing agendas in the nation today. An agenda that includes the privatization of schools, an end to early education, return to the death penalty, a law prohibiting Sharia Law, the passage of a bill that declared Christianity the state's religion, elimination of the state's income and corporate tax rates, disenfranchisement of minority voters and aggressive anti-abortion legislation. In a state where liberals equal the number of conservatives, North Carolina appears more and more like a Christian-Corporate Theocracy.

So with the nation ever more tilting left, how are our elective bodies and courts swinging so hard to the far right? Like everything else in life, it's a case of follow the cashola. And where the flow of money from big corporations and billionaires leads, at least politically, is directly to the feet of the Christian Right.

Now, this book isn't an endorsement of the Democratic Party or any political party, for there is any number of reasons to be disappointed in Obama and the Democratic Party in general. Democrats have been on the wrong side of history and the wrong side of the will of the American people in times past. How can we forget the whole slavery thing? But today it's the Republican Party and its drivers that are on the wrong side of justice. The arc of the universe is long but for now, it doesn't bend towards Ted Cruz. Thus, this book is an appeal to atheists, secularists and free thinkers to awaken and mobilize against the most dangerous threat to American democracy today: the plutocratic sponsorship of the Christian Right. While that looks and sounds a lot like the Koch brother funded Tea Party, it runs deeper than that. It's a strategy to control state and federal legislatures, and the courts – in a way that says, "We don't care what the people want. We write the laws, and those laws will not reflect the wishes of the centre majority but will cater only for the fanatical Christian Right and its corporate cronies." In other words, where plutocracy and theocracy come to mate. The genius of the plutocratic-theocratic game lies in its simplicity. Its success lies with a largely apathetic electorate, a dysfunctional media and an ill informed religious base that resides mostly in the South. Corporate elites represent less than 0.01 percent of the electorate, but 300,000 voters don't win you many national elections. Further, the economic interests of the bottom 90 percent of the country are not aligned with the economic and social interests of the top 0.1 percent. So how do Wall Street, the Koch brothers, Rupert Murdoch, Donald Trump, and the rich assholes of the OC get white people earning under $80,000 per year to vote for an economic agenda that benefits only those in the top 0.1 percent echelon? The answer is Jesus. Not the Jesus of the Bible, however, that Jesus was a liberal Jew who gave away free healthcare, booze, and hung with a prostitute. I'm talking about an even more fictional Jesus – supply side economics and white power Jesus. Who happens to be a fictional character based loosely on a fictional character. He looks like biblical Jesus but sounds like President Reagan on a good day and Jessie Helms on a bad day.

The corporate elite has convinced the highly religious struggling white middle class that today's economic problems and stresses are exclusively the end result of decades of government handouts to the "moocher class," alongside the erosion of traditional Christian values. In other words, the erroneous belief that government has taken their tax dollars and given it away to non-working blacks and Latinos ("the bad Christians") in the form of handouts and entitlements. It's the perfect scapegoat and without a doubt a strategically robust plan. If the corporate elite can sit back and watch the middle class blame the underclass, and each other, then the agenda and the sins of the wealthy elite gets a free ride. In short, its propaganda is no more sophisticated than the Nazis blaming Germany's societal ills on the Jews.

By marginalizing the poor as "moochers", and trumpeting the top 1 percent as "job creators", the Christian Right, which is predominantly middle class, has championed political stooges of big business into political offices throughout the land, thus paving the way for the pummeling of unions, slashing of taxes on the rich, promotion of outsourcing jobs abroad, the monopolization of industries, reduction in real median wage, and the deregulation of Wall Street.

So, what has been the price?

In terms of total number of billionaires, America ranks number one in the Western world. A better measure of economic societal health, however, is median wealth. On that, we now rank #27. We have fallen so far in the past three decades that we now trail a number of little countries that most Republicans cannot locate on a map, like Cyprus, Qatar, New Zealand, Spain, and Ireland. And even Kuwait! Yes, we have lower median wealth than an Arabian state that we had to save from a Third World dictator, Saddam Hussein.

Social and income inequality is now the major issue of our time. A mere 400 Americans own 50 percent of this nation's wealth.

The American dream has become a real life nightmare for all but the elite few. The American dream is a notion that anybody, regardless of background, can achieve financial stability and build a secure life for his or her family – and this dream is a huge part of this country's self-identity. But, as the late, great George Carlin said, "The American dream: you have to be asleep to believe it."

The fact that 26 countries now rank above us in terms of realizing that dream of financial stability should serve as a wake up call that things have gotten real shitty in a short period of time. That we rank behind countries that are generally recognized as abysmal economies, Ireland (18), Spain (20), and Cyprus (25), should be enough to jolt us from the deepest of slumbers, but I guess we are too distracted watching *The Bachelorette*.

Why has our way of life tumbled so low? Former Secretary of Commerce under President Clinton, Robert Reich, says, "Although the output of Americans has continued to rise, almost all the gains have gone to the very top." This is no accident. This is by design. This is what we are left with after three decades of the trickle down myth, which ushered in three decades of financial deregulation, which has concentrated wealth at the top of the income pyramid. Wage stagnation has made life harder for working families. And the shredding of America's social safety net has made it nearly impossible for people to climb out of poverty. Reich adds, "Four decades ago, the typical household's income rose in tandem with output. But since the late 1970s, as these laws took hold, most Americans' incomes have flattened. Had the real median household income continued to keep pace with economic growth it would now be almost $92,000 instead of $50,000."

At the risk of being accused of self-indulgent hyperbole, we can attribute the gigantic socio-economic mess this country now finds itself entirely at the feet of social conservative Christians, thus making the Christian Right the single largest threat to the American way of life today. The Christian Right has unwittingly escorted the policies of the rich and big business into our laws, and now we are all paying the price. I will come back to this point in more detail, but first let's quantify how far American society has fallen.

Despite what you hear on Fox & Friends, and every other talking head in the right wing echo chamber, America is no longer the #1 country in the world; nor is it the greatest experiment of democracy ever. "American exceptionalism" is nothing more than a self-serving, right wing generated myth. America is something that can no longer be boasted of. Wrap your mind around some of the following facts. The USA is ranked:

- #7 in literacy
- #27 in math
- #22 in science
- #34 in life expectancy
- #35 in infant mortality
- #27 in median wealth

Further, not a single American city is included in the top 10 most livable cities in the world. Only one American airport is listed in the top 100 airports in the world. Our roads, schools and bridges are literally falling apart or collapsing into the rivers below them. Despite being the richest country in the world, nearly a quarter of Americans (24 percent) say they had trouble putting food on the table in the past 12 months. This is up from just 16 percent who reported such deprivation in 2007, the year before the Great Recession began.

Our sense of food insecurity is more on par with that experienced by Indonesians and Tanzanians than it is with Australians or Canadians. In fact, the percentage of Americans who say they could not afford the food needed by their families at some point in the last year is three times that in Germany, more than twice that in Italy and Canada.

As you can see, our way of life is the envy only of the most dysfunctional backwaters around the globe.

Mind you, we do lead the world in some categories for which we can proudly boast:

- #1 in incarcerated citizens per capita
- #1 in military spending, where we spend 40 times what the next 10 countries spend combined.
- #2 in children living in extreme poverty
- #1 in obesity
- #1 in teen pregnancy among OECD countries
- #1 in the number of adults who believe angels are real
- #1 in the number of adults who believe Noah's Ark is how the earth re-populated

By any measure we have fallen so very far as a great country, and the breadth of our demise is summarized brilliantly by Aaron Sorkin's tele-drama *Newsroom*. In the first episode of the first season, the character Will McEvoy, as played by Jeff Daniels, says to a room full of college students:

> We sure used to be (the greatest country in the world). We stood up for what was right. We fought for moral reasons. We passed laws, struck down laws, for moral reasons. We waged wars on poverty, not poor people. We sacrificed. We cared about our neighbors. We put our money where our mouths were. And we never beat our chest.
>
> We built great big things, made ungodly technological advances, explored the universe, cured diseases, and we cultivated the world's greatest artists and the world's greatest economy. We reached for the stars. Acted like men.
>
> We aspired to intelligence. We didn't belittle education, and science didn't make us feel inferior.
>
> We didn't identify ourselves by who we voted for in the last election, and we didn't, oh, we didn't scare so easy. Ha. We were able to be all these things and do all these things because we were informed. By great men. Men who were revered. First step in solving any problem is recognizing there is one. America is not the greatest country in the world anymore.

So where did things go so horribly wrong? Well, the top 1 percent, the plutocratic elite, figured out how to get more than 50 percent of the remaining 99 percent of the country to vote for the interests of the top 1 percent, particularly in local and state elections. The plutocratic elite figured a way to convince low to middle income wage earners to vote for the proxy of big business. They figured out a way to get a voter struggling to survive on $7 per hour to vote for the party that fights to keep the minimum wage at $7 per hour. They figured out a way to get a voter who lacks health coverage to vote for a party that wants to deny them health coverage. I could go on, but the point is this – it's superstitious belief in God that keeps these bottom 50 percent income earners, the low-information Jesus freaks, pulling the lever for the top 1 percent at the ballot box.

It's no wonder the doctrine of trickle down economics, a doctrine solely to the benefit of the richest 1 percent, was ushered into prominence at the same time as the birth of social conservatism. Both trickle down economics and social conservatism were launched upon the American electorate with the so-called Reagan Revolution in 1981. This began the period of deregulation; the shrinking of government; and the birth of frightened Christian wedge politics. Politicians on the right would fight for the interests of the elite, but would need the support of the uninformed at the polls to implement their anti-regulation, anti-taxation, pro-special interest agenda. For the elites to attain their fiscal objectives they would need to, cynically, get behind the ideology of Christian social conservatives. An ideology that can be expressed as:

- Advancing pro-life and anti-abortion stances on unwanted or unplanned pregnancies
- Advocating traditional marriage and a ban on gay marriage
- Eliminating federal funding for embryonic stem-cell research and finding alternative methods of research
- Protecting the Second Amendment right to bear arms

- Maintaining a strong national defense
- Protecting US economic interests against foreign threats, and eliminating the need for trade unions
- Opposing immigration
- Limiting welfare spending for America's needy
- Lifting the ban on school prayer
- Implementing high tariffs on countries that do not uphold human rights
- Supporting war on drugs

During the middle two-thirds of the 20th century, the U.S. experienced a strong and activist Federal government, starting from FDR's New Deal through to the start of the Reagan presidency. In the last two generations, and particularly under the two Bush presidencies, the Republican Party acted to both restrict the power of Congress and the courts in favor of a reinvigorated "states' rights". The focus on states' rights was ostensibly intended to "return power to the people" by reining in the "morally zealous and apparently unconstitutional" actions of the Federal government. In reality, however, states' rights have meant the weakening of rights and protections of citizens in favor of a religiously conservative social and economically corporate-dominated agenda.

It's a pitiful irony that those states under permanent Republican control, thanks to the enduring support of religious conservative voters, are the states with the most individual suffering. Take Mississippi, for example, the most Christian state in the Union, where 32 percent of its children suffer in extreme poverty. In New Mexico, another reliable conservative state, 31 percent of kids live in extreme poverty. In both states, the primary reason for abject poverty is that more than a third of the state's children have parents who lack secure employment, decent wages, and healthcare. But thanks to Jesus, these poor saps vote for the party who reject Medicaid expansion, oppose early education expansion, legislate larger cuts to education, slash food stamps to make room for oil and agriculture subsidies on top of tax cuts and loopholes for corporations and the wealthy.

The case of Mississippi and New Mexico are not isolated examples. The bottom five worst states in terms of children living in extreme poverty are rounded out by Arizona, Nevada, and Louisiana. Other than having Republican state legislatures, what do these five states share in common? All these states, save New Mexico, enacted right to work laws that funnel more people into poverty as a result of creating pathetically low wage conditions, while corporations in each state are thriving with record levels of profits. Two of the states, Mississippi and Louisiana, have rejected Medicaid expansion. Political news site PoliticsUsa.com points out:

> In all, there are 13 states not participating in the free expansion (of Medicaid) and six others leaning toward non-participation and, to no-one's surprise, all 19 states are Republican-controlled and more than pleased to prevent millions of their residents, especially children, from benefiting from the most basic healthcare provisions. From a Republican perspective, it likely makes sense to keep the poorest, and youngest, residents in ill-health to go along with daily hunger to round out an existence steeped in suffering and despair.

Nine of the top ten poorest states are found in the South. Thompson writes, "It's a region [the South] that stands out from the nation at large for its slavish devotion to economic policies that increase the burden on its poor, rather than allowing its lower and working classes to share in the financial harvest that its politicians and business leaders are so eager to tout in speeches." A book titled *Taxing the Poor* looks at the way we tax the poor in the United States, particularly in the South, where poor families are often subject to income taxes, and where regressive sales taxes apply even to food for home consumption. The authors, Newman and O'Brien, write:

> The legacy of the past – southern opposition to property taxation in the nineteenth century – continues to define the disparity in tax structure and revenue we see today....That legacy has cost the southern states dearly [and] is placing a heavy burden on the rest of the country as well. The pattern is distinctive and destructive. The problem is very much with us today in part because....very high barriers to change are in place throughout the South and have been for decades.

All this despair comes courtesy of low information voters being duped by the corporate elite to vote against their own economic self-interest. The corporate elite and their political appointees have convinced tens of millions of Americans that a vote against stem-cell research is more important to a Christian's needs than a vote against cuts in education spending, food stamp reductions, the elimination of school lunches and the abolition of healthcare programs.

Big money has allowed right wing politicians to get away with shifting economic blame to the poor. Creating jobs should be the top economic priority, but the Republican base focuses excessively on deficit reduction. It's no secret that social wedge issues are used by the Right to drive low-income people to the polls. The point is that in an overly religious country it works too well, and to America's detriment. Pushing sophisticated tax schemes for already wealthy venture capitalists, like the 16 percent tax rate Mitt Romney gets away with, doesn't excite the base. On the other hand, "taking back the country" from the gay socialist Muslim Kenyan liberal Marxist agenda does, as do issues like abortion, and stopping sodomy. The Right's passion for these social issues often makes them the loudest in these debates, and the sheer volume, which is amplified through the right wing echo chambers, makes progressives limit themselves. We tend to believe we represent the minority. We don't! A majority of Americans support the rich paying a greater share of the tax burden, better gun control laws, access to family planning, and the like. The fact is that while the Christian Right believes it represents the "real America", it does not. They are now the minority, and they are on the way out entirely. *But* they are winning, and they are making America in their own image. Progressives must avoid the temptation of allowing America's changing demographics to win these battles for us. By then it will be too late. We need to engage our cultural opponents on their turf, and restore the *real* traditional American values as envisioned by the Founding Fathers. Not the warped, revisionist right wing Confederacy version of history.

There's a reason the word "corporation" doesn't appear anywhere in the Constitution. After fighting a revolution to free themselves from control by English corporations, the Founding Fathers retained a healthy fear of corporate power. Corporations were forbidden from attempting to influence elections and public policy. The nation's governing blueprint does read as Separation of Corporation and State. Equally, the founders of this nation had an even greater mistrust of organized religion and thus went to great lengths to ensure that Separation of Church and State would be the Constitution's firewall. But all this is under attack by a corporate sponsored, religious conservative agenda.

This book is an examination of how corporations and the Christian Right are winning, and a road map for what secularists and free thinkers will need to do to overcome this highly dangerous and formidable foe.

ELECTIONS HAVE CONSEQUENCES

"Elections are won by men and women chiefly because most people vote against somebody rather than for somebody."

FRANKLIN P. ADAMS

After squeaking out victory against the politically wood-ened candidate John Kerry in the 2004 election, President George Walker Bush stood before the deliriously delighted Republican faithful and declared, "Elections have conse-quences." While rarely commended for his elocution or use of the English language, Bush's headline-grabbing statement was trenchant. Translated, it means that follow-ing elections, the winners get to govern how they see fit. When applied to the 2012 election, Bush's aphorism held even greater meaning, for the contest between Obama and Romney presented a stark contrast on which direction Americans wished to see the country headed. Both major parties laid out clear and starkly contrasting visions: the Republican Party's philosophy of, "You're on your own," versus the Democrat Party's, "We are in this together."

After scoring a resounding victory in the 2010 mid-terms, thanks largely to the mobilization of the Christian Right under the Tea Party banner, the Republican Party blocked President Obama at every turn during the second-half of his first term, pulling the nation sharply to the right in the process. The 2012 presidential contest offered the GOP a clear shot at controlling all three branches of government. Moreover, it provided an opportunity for the loony right wing extremists, the nihilists, zealots, and know-nothings to repeal the entirety of the social compact that dated all the way back to the New Deal.

A majority of voters pay scant attention to the whims of political discourse and the machinations of Washington D.C. We have jobs to do, kids to raise, and porn to download. The only time most of us tune into the political conversation is when it's time to vote. And even then our vote is based largely on how the candidate makes us feel about ourselves. Why? Because most of us are idiots!

But in the end, when the election goes the way we hoped, we feel a small sense of satisfaction that our civic duty helped shaped history. But more often than not, that small afterglow is replaced not long after with a returning cynicism towards D.C. and everything that goes on there. Our cynicism, however, is typically a by-product of not understanding how things work and our ever-widening collective attention deficit disorders. That's a nice necklace. Where did you buy it? Look, Paris Hilton fucked a pool boy. I like robots. What was my point about cynicism?

During the 2012 election campaign, I read and listened to a whole host of armchair pundits who were saying they were likely to sit out this election because they felt Obama "let them down" or "didn't deliver on his promise of hope and change." People were saying this a mere 100 days into his presidency! Look, "Hope" was a one-syllable slogan, it wasn't even as much as a PowerPoint presentation. Change takes time. The Civil Rights movement fought bigotry and discrimination for decades before the country realized change that was righteous. The fight to change Washington, the fight to save this democracy from becoming a full-blown plutocracy infused with theocracy, will take time, too. And it will take more than one politician and one term to do it. Comedian Rob Delaney posted on Twitter: "Obama let you down? Blow it out your ass. He's a multi-millionaire career politician who doesn't know you exist, you sissy, but he might be the reason your grandkids have health insurance."

Ultimately, the bottom line is this: very few people knew what was on the line during the 2012 election. For most, it was a contest of likeability. A great percentage of the votes went to Obama based solely on the fact people saw Romney as a creepy rich dude with an even creepier tie to the creepiest of religious cults – the Mormon Church. But very few saw what was at stake here. And what was at stake was the American democratic system. Hyperbole, sure! So let's talk to this point a little more.

With the Republican Party holding just one of the three branches of government, the House, the country has paid an enormous price for the short time the most extreme elements of the GOP have held control of the legislative branch. We saw our credit rating downgraded; we saw not a single jobs bills passed at a time when the economy needed it most – instead we got more than three dozen failed attempts to repeal the Affordable Care Act; we saw the groundwork for the eventual sequestration, which cut funding to the poor and much needed infrastructures like schools, roads, and bridges. So imagine if the religiously conservative social and economically corporate-dominated agenda held sway over all three branches of government? Which was the reality the country faced going into the 2012 election. That kind of end-to-end political control would ensure that everything we have achieved as a society would end up being repealed; and everything we hoped to achieve in the future would be taken out with an ideological pre-emptive strike.

In short, a win to Romney would have meant the following:

1. Making the wealthy even wealthier by implementing tax cuts, which ultimately remove the safety nets for everyone else.

2. Turning Americans against each other: Native Americans against immigrants; middle class against the poor; non-union versus union; young versus old.

3. Substituting private morality for public morality. In other words, deflect attention away from corporate predatory practices and shift it towards who we can and can't fuck; who we can and can't marry; "illegitimate" rape; contraception. In other words, if we're talking about what private citizens do in the privacy of their own bedrooms, then we won't pay attention to the immoralities taking place inside the privacy of corporate boardrooms, such as outsourcing jobs; exploitation of tax loopholes; unconscionable conduct; defrauding investors and consumers.

4. The elimination of safety nets such as Medicare, Medicaid, social security, and unemployment insurance.

5. A regressive tax system that only benefits the rich and hurts the poor, thus widening the already gaping income inequality.

In particular, a Romney win would have meant the Paul Ryan budget became law. Now, if you've got better things to do than read a 10,000-page fiscal policy document, let me provide you with everything you need to know in 16 words or less: the Paul Ryan budget would kill tens of thousands of Americans each and every year, and that's just the start of it.

How so? The Ryan budget meant killing the Affordable Care Act and crippling Medicare and Medicaid. And the more people who lack health coverage, the more people who die. How many people are we talking about? The estimates of people who will die as a result of being uninsured vary, from 500 to 1,000 for every one million who lack coverage. Repealing the Affordable Care Act alone would deny promised coverage for 32 million Americans, which would mean somewhere from 16,000 to 32,000 meeting a premature death each year.

Then there's Ryan's proposal to replace Medicare with vouchers to buy private insurance. This is a cynical attempt to cook the books in a way that shifts costs from the federal government, and, in turn, assigns it to the seniors and the disabled who are covered by Medicare. The nonpartisan Congressional Budget Office (CBO) reported that the Ryan voucher plan would have doubled the already high cost of health care to seniors. Meaning – they will become sicker.

In short, the Ryan budget is arguably the most radical policy blueprint to come out of Washington in a half-century. Even the nefarious right-wing extremist Newt Gingrich called it "radical right-wing social engineering," which is like Alex Rodriguez calling Lance Armstrong a drug cheat. Worse, the proposed cuts in discretionary spending would've been devastating, with everything from medical and scientific research to food stamps and college loans facing the prospect of cuts to the tune of 40 to

50 percent. In total, almost two-thirds of the Ryan cuts came from programs directed at the poor. Jonathon Alter writes, "It simultaneously shredded the social safety net, swept away the country's seed corn of investments in the future, and adopted a discredited supply-side economics."

In a May 2012 speech at George Washington University, President Obama said Ryan's budget "would lead to a fundamentally different America than the one we've known" and called it, "changing of the basic social compact in America."

It's no secret that one of the central reasons the Romney campaign believed Ryan to be the ideal running mate was because of his appeal to the Christian conservative base of the Republican Party. Ryan is a devout Catholic and has said his policies are "rooted in his Christian beliefs" – not only his positions against homosexuality and abortion but also on government spending and entitlements for the poor. But it's funny how I can't find anywhere in the Bible where Jesus called the poor "moochers" or where Jesus said, "Fuck off, this bread is mine!"

You see, like all Christian fundamentalists who believe the world to be a mere 7,000 years old, Ryan has trouble with simple arithmetic, and thus his budget would not only destroy the poor but would prolong the country's recession, or worse – push it into a deep depression. Someone who does understand numbers and math, however, is Nobel Laureate winning economist Paul Krugman, who wrote:

> He (Ryan) is, in fact, a big fraud, who doesn't care at all about fiscal responsibility, and whose policy proposals are sloppy as well as dishonest. Of

course, this means that he'll fit in to the Romney campaign just fine.

He's a hard-core conservative, with a voting record as far right as Michelle Bachman's [sic], who has shown no competence at all on the numbers thing.

Mr. Ryan has somehow acquired a reputation as a stern fiscal hawk despite offering budget proposals that, far from being focused on deficit reduction, are mainly about cutting taxes for the rich while slashing aid to the poor and unlucky.

Last year, when Paul Ryan first made a big splash with his budget proposal, many commentators – some of them pretending to be moderates or at any rate only moderate conservatives – lavished praise on its fiscal responsibility. Then people who actually know how to read budget numbers weighed in, revealing it as a piece of mean-spirited junk.

The bottom-line is this was a budget the Romney campaign ran on. This was to be the Republican fiscal blueprint to run the country for the next eight plus years. But it was a budget based on ideological dreams and trickle down fairy wand-waving. A plan where the numbers are just made up, with the cynical reassurance that the media, in their desperate desire to remain neutral, are terrified of calling out political bullshit these days. In fact, the numbers are based in so little reality that it led to the CBO stating that the Ryan budget would only serve to increase the deficit over the coming years. Krugman wrote, "The plan's a fraud. The plan is a big bunch of tax cuts, some specified spending cuts, basically for poor people, and then a huge magic asterisk, which is supposed to turn into a deficit reduction plan, but, in fact, if you look what's actually in it, it's a deficit-increasing plan."

But facts and reality are not something the Christian Right is interested in. Obviously! You know, heaven and talking donkeys. They simply don't care, and more often than not are too stupid to understand. The corporate sponsors of the GOP don't care for good governance either; you know things like balancing a federal budget or actually running a country. They care only that their taxes are lowered, despite taxes being at a nearly 90 year low on the top tax brackets, and that regulations like environmental standards are obliterated, and things like workplace laws and wages resemble that of a Chinese factory. That's not hyperbole. In fact, when Scott Prouty, the waiter who secretly filmed Romney's infamous "47 percent" remarks, released his video recording to online political blog *Mother Jones*, he had assumed that the most damaging self-inflicting wounds made by the Republican candidate were the ones that had to do with American owned Chinese sweat shops, like the ones Mitt Romney owns:

> Back in my private equity days, we went to China to buy a factory there. It employed about twenty thousand people and they were almost all young women between the ages of about eighteen to twenty-two or twenty-three. They were saving for potentially becoming married, and they work in these huge factories that make very small appliances. And we were walking through these facilities, seeing them work, the numbers of hours they work per day, the pittance they earn, living in dormitories with little bathrooms at the end. The rooms, they had ten or twelve girls per room – three bunk beds on top of

each other....And around the factory was a huge fence with barbed wires and guard towers. And we said, "Gosh! I can't believe you, you know, keep these girls in!" They said, "No, no, no. This is to keep other people from coming in."

The barbed wire and guard towers were to keep people out? Who was he kidding? Prouty said afterwards, "I heard zero empathy in his voice for anybody. I looked around the room to see if anyone else was disgusted, and no one seemed to be. Romney's tone was, 'Isn't that wonderful that we can share this with the world?' Share this? I said to myself, If this guy is running the show, he's a danger – almost a sociopath." The ultimate point being this: if Romney thought the Chinese factory was a good business model to invest his own money in, then is he saying this is fine for America, too?

Ultimately, the corporate-driven end game is to make the entire nation look like the South. Year after year, decade after decade, the South votes for policies that do not support their own economic self-interests. Again, this is because of Jesus H Christ! To quote Chuck Thompson yet again, he notes that whites in the South overwhelmingly support right-to-work laws, which Thompson defines, correctly, as "the Orwellian euphemism for the 'right for companies to disregard the welfare of their workers.'" According to a 2009 survey by Grand Valley State University, annual salaries for autoworkers in Alabama, Tennessee and South Carolina averaged about $55,400, while their counterparts in Michigan averaged $74,500. Thompson notes that Southern blue-collar workers also have "inferior health and pension plans, less job security, higher risk of being fired for trivial reasons, and diminished safety precautions…"

Not only are Southern workers hurt by their anti-union attitudes, the whole nation suffers, too. "Southern economic success," writes Thompson, "comes at the expense of the rest of the country." He asks, "Everyone has joked about a modern-day secession. Politicians, like Texas Governor and presidential hopeful Rick Perry, have even threatened it. But what would the measurable impact be if it actually happened? Well, with time, Americans would start thinking of the South as another Mexico, only with a more corrupt government."

Now forget what you hear about the South (and its red states) being anti-government spending. It's bullshit, but many of its deep fried food-worshipping citizens don't even realize it. They don't realize that they're far more dependent on federal government spending than the progressive blue states. In fact, the South is home to 9 of the nation's 10 poorest states and all of its states get far more in government subsidies than they pay out in taxes. As an illustration, let's compare the reliably blue state of New Jersey with the staunch red state of Kentucky. New Jersey gets back 70 cents for every dollar in taxes it sends to the federal government. Kentucky, on the other hand, receives $1.57 for every buck it pays. The added irony, as if this point needed any further irony, is that Rand Paul is the Senator for Kentucky. Yes, the Libertarian, who believes every government department should be replaced by the church, and bemoans every dollar the government spends on education and healthcare. Yes, these are facts you will not hear on Fox & Friends. The old adage applies: "We love fiscal discipline unless it's our stuff."

Essentially, and contrary to the claims in Obama's 2008 nomination speech, there really are two Americas. We are two countries pretending to be one. We have irreconcilable differences on health care, abortion laws, same-sex marriage, gun control, voter registration, education subsidies, the role of religion in society, the definition of patriotism, and the role of unions. Southerners want the federal government to stop spending money and get out of their lives. If the South were to secede, then we in the blue states would pay lower taxes because we would no longer have to support the poorest states in the country.

Given secession is unlikely to happen, however, thanks largely to the South's dependence on federal spending (moochers), the end-game for the religiously conservative social and economically corporate-dominated agenda is for the entire nation to look like the religious South. That way, the big corporations can pay lower taxes, which results in wiping out services for the poor; lower wages without union interference; lower environmental protection, which pollutes our water and skies;

Unsurprisingly, however, rank-and-file Southern voters – who have lower average incomes than other Americans – resoundingly defeated Obama in the 2008 election. In fact, the eventual president carried no more than 14 percent of the white vote in Alabama, Mississippi, and Louisiana. No-one expected Obama to win these states in 2012, but the point here is to emphasize the blowback that falls on these voters who cast votes for the Republican Party purely on religious ideological lines.

Indeed, elections have consequences. The consequences were so high in 2012 because they cut to the heart of the American experiment. This election clearly defined the

Right's agenda, with that being to allow extreme partisan distortions to define our policy debates and thus paralyze our capacity for constructive self-government. Not satisfied with already having stolen the economic security of most Americans, the tiny minority, the CEOs on Wall Street, is doing everything it can to prevent the majority from reclaiming its economic rights.

The corporate elite and the GOP continue to proselytize "trickle down" economics, even though that theory has been proven a complete failure wherever it has been tried. The GOP policies of cut taxes at any cost and then implement austerity for the poor and middle class has been an abject disaster throughout Europe. During the July 2013 meeting of the G-20 finance ministers, there was a clear consensus on the need for an effective stimulus in order to spark economic growth, and broad agreement that austerity has been a failure and should be rejected. Well, Europe, Paul Krugman told you so! The *New York Times* reported that, "Most governments see recovery as too weak to risk reduced spending on unemployment benefits, job training, education, and other public sector outlays. The debate between growth and austerity seems to have come to an end." But don't tell that to the Republican Party who continue to pass the most radical cuts in critical investments in a generation. Despite the fact that Fed Chairman Bernanke testified before Congress that the greatest threat to the recovery were attempts in Congress to slash spending investments that are critical to our economic growth.

For the past three decades, the nation's economic policies have been, for the most part, authored by Wall Street and the politicians who legislate these policies into law, and the results are in.

For the years 1977 to 2010, the wealth of the top 1 percent increased by 281 percent, whereas the wealth of the middle class grew by 16 percent. In that same period, the incomes of CEOs grew by 726 percent, whereas the average worker's income grew by just 5.7 percent. Are there any questions? This is the result of the Christian Right electing Republican politicians who only care for one winner: the super rich. If you still need convincing, consider the data President Clinton drew upon during his keynote address for the 2012 Democratic National Convention. He said, "Since 1961, for 52 years now, the Republicans have held the White House 28 years, the Democrats 24. In those 52 years, our private economy has produced 66 million private-sector jobs. So what's the jobs score? Republicans 24 million, Democrats 42 million."

So is Clinton's claim accurate? According to the Bureau of Labor Statistics, here are the net increases in private-sector employment under each president, chronologically by party:

REPUBLICANS

Richard Nixon:	Increase of 7.1 million jobs
Gerald Ford:	Increase of 1.3 million jobs
Ronald Reagan:	Increase of 14.7 million jobs
George H.W. Bush:	Increase of 1.5 million jobs
George W. Bush:	Decline of 646,000 jobs

**Total: Increase of 23.9 million jobs
under Republican presidents**

DEMOCRATS

John F. Kennedy:	Increase of 2.7 million jobs
Lyndon B. Johnson:	Increase of 9.5 million jobs
Jimmy Carter:	Increase of 9.0 million jobs
Bill Clinton:	Increase of 20.8 million jobs
Barack Obama:	Increase of 332,000 jobs

**Total: Increase of 42.3 million jobs
under Democrat presidents**

One cannot overstate how dramatically the above figures underscore true economic realities. Namely, that when economic principles that favor the middle class are implemented, the entire economy grows. When the middle class has more to spend, companies hire more workers to meet the demand. Consider that today U.S. corporations sit on a record $2 trillion cash, but are not creating meaningful new jobs. The reasons they're not creating jobs is the middle class isn't growing or spending. In other words, the theory of cutting taxes and spending to create jobs is complete baloney. If you doubt that, please refer to President Clinton's job scoreboard.

CHAPTER TWO

ELECTIONS FOR SALE

> "A handful of billionaires own a significant part of the wealth of America and have enormous control over our economy. What the Supreme Court did in Citizens United is to say to these same billionaires: 'You own and control the economy, you own Wall Street, you own the coal companies, you own the oil companies. Now, for a very small percentage of your wealth, we're going to give you the opportunity to own the United States government.'"
>
> **SEN. BERNIE SANDERS**

Not all that long ago, elections generally reflected the will of the people. Also not that long ago, it was possible to find Republican politicians who were not merely puppets of corporations and big business. In fact, it was a Republican president who was so troubled by the growing influence of corporate money over the outcome of elections, that first enacted laws to ban unlimited corporate donations. That Republican was President Theodore Roosevelt, and in 1907 he paved the way for the passing of the Tillman Act, named for its sponsor Senator Benjamin Tillman, which put a ban on corporate contributions. This Act sought to:

- Limit the influence of wealthy individuals and special interest groups on the outcome of federal elections;
- Regulate spending in campaigns for federal office; and
- Deter abuses by mandating public disclosure of campaign finances.

In 1971, under the Federal Election Campaign Act (FECA), the Tillman Act was further consolidated, with Congress instituting more stringent disclosure requirements for candidates, parties, and political action committees (PACs). Further, Congress established the income tax checkoff to provide for the financing of presidential elections.

The presidential election campaign fund checkoff appeared on U.S. income tax return forms as a question: "Do you want $3 of your federal tax to go to the Presidential Election Campaign Fund?" This money is then distributed equally to both the Republican and Democratic nominees in the general election. A candidate from a third party or an independent is illegible to receive this public funding in the event they receive more than five percent of the vote. Also, smaller funds are allocated to candidates in the respective party's primary process. The campaign fund reduces a candidate's dependence on large contributions from individuals and special-interest groups.

This is how it works:

- The fund will match every dollar a candidate raises from individual donors. For example, let's say I'm running to be the Democratic nominee for the 2016 general election. If one of my supporters donates $20 to my campaign, then the fund will match that with a $20 donation to my campaign. The fund will match a maximum of $250 per individual donation.

- A candidate must first establish eligibility by submitting to the Federal Election Commission (FEC) proof that at least $5000 was raised in each of at least 20 states.
- The spending limit for the primary election is $40.9 million, of which a candidate must abide by state limits of 65.4 cents per person of voting age population in a state, or $817,800, whichever is greater.
- In the general election, the respective presidential nominee of each major party becomes eligible for a public grant of $81.78 million. To be eligible for the grant, however, the candidate must not accept private contributions to the campaign.

This is the way elections should be financed. This lays the turf for hosting the hallmark of our democracy: free and open elections with a peaceful transition of power. Yes, certainly loopholes allowed for unlimited donations to the Democratic National Committee (DNC) and Republican National Committee (RNC), but this mostly empowered donors contributing or bundling donations in the tens of thousands of dollars, not tens of millions.

But then something really bad happened in 2010. Enter the political action group, Citizens United. On the surface, the two words put together, citizens-united, sounds innocuous enough, right? So who are they? This excerpt is taken directly from their website:

> Citizens United is an organization dedicated to restoring our government to citizens' control. Through a combination of education, advocacy, and grass roots organization, Citizens United seeks to reassert the traditional American values of lim-

ited government, freedom of enterprise, strong families, and national sovereignty and security. Citizens United's goal is to restore the Founding Fathers' vision of a free nation, guided by the honesty, common sense, and good will of its citizens.

Grass roots, advocacy, strong families, security, and yada yada yada leaves you with the impression it's a bunch of like-minded neighbors coming together to push for things that make their communities stronger. All good home-grown stuff, right? Well, that's what *they* would like you to believe, especially the part about it being a grassroots organization. So who are they? They'd be the second wealthiest citizens in the land. In terms of total wealth, they're just a few dollars shy of Bill Gates and a few bucks in front of Warren Buffet. Please allow me to introduce you to the brothers Charles and David Koch. (Apparently it's pronounced *Coke*, but I don't believe them.) Forbes estimates their combined wealth to exceed $50billion, which is exceeded only by the Microsoft founder's $59 billion fortune. The Koch Empire is built on a petrochemical company founded by their father. They own refineries, pipelines, paper mills, synthetic fiber factories, and chemical plants. After Cargill, they are the second largest private company in the United States with $115 billion in revenues and more than 60,000 employees. But before you leap to anoint them "job creators", know this: 43 percent of their current wealth ($15 billion) was accumulated by aggressive speculative trading on volatile energy markets in the years between 2010 and 2013. Their wealth now equals the combined GDP of no fewer than 85 countries. In fact, their amassed fortune equals 88 times the GDP of Samoa. Interestingly, the Koch brothers' story clearly dispels the "job creator" myth. For while they have amassed 43 percent of the fortune on speculative trading, which depends on employing no one, they have laid off tens of thousands of workers across dozens of companies during the few years they funneled $15 billion into their Swiss bank accounts. MSNBC host Rachel Maddow says, "The more money they seem to make, the less people they are employing." A fact that is illustrative of the problems with corporations at large in America today. At the risk of sidetracking a little, corporations are seeing profits grow 20 percent year on year, but these profits are not translating into jobs for Americans. Thus putting to rest the lie that is central to the GOP's argument that taxing corporations and rich people will stunt job growth.

The Koch brothers have a very straightforward agenda: to destroy social security, public education, and eliminate the minimum wage. The messengers of their agenda are the numerous think tanks they sponsor, the politicians they pay, the universities they own or are major benefactors of, and the pundits who disseminate their distortions on right leaning media outlets.

They are the chief architects of the right wing misinformation campaign. They pay their pundits to get on television and spread mass distortions of reality. You will hear the politicians who are in their pocket say, "Social Security is going bankrupt." Fact: Social Security has a $2.7 trillion surplus. You will hear Fox News hosts use the Koch funded think tank talking points, such as, "We need to raise retirement age" ; "We need to eliminate the minimum wage". The Koch brothers contributed more than $500,000 to members of the House Energy & Commerce Committee, making them the single largest contributor to that committee. The result? Congress continues to kill environmental protection regulation, which benefits them. They benefit from lower energy production costs. But that in no way benefits America.

A provocative documentary *The Koch Brothers Exposed*, directed by Robert Greenwald, who notably uncovered unethical labor practices at Wal-Mart, was released in 2013. Greenwald writes, "The Kochs are using their money, their power and the inequalities of our system for personal gain, and the size and scale that they're doing it is fairly impressive." The documentary's official press release provided a full list of the documentary's findings"

- The Echo Chamber of Influence – Documents and interviews unearthed by Brave New Foundation researchers illustrate a28.4 million Koch effort that has manufactured 297 opinions and commentaries, 200 reports, 56 studies and six books distorting Social Security's effectiveness and purpose. This is just one example of the vast industry comprised of Koch brothers' spokespeople, front groups, think tanks, academics and elected officials, which has built a self-sustaining echo chamber to transform fringe ideas into popular mainstream public policy arguments.
- Voter Suppression – Through their web of political influence, the Kochs' have bought access to democracy's lifeblood: free and fair elections. The Kochs' have funded efforts to thwart 21 million Americans from voting as Koch dollars helped write and propose voting suppression bills in 38 states.
- Re-Segregation – Americans for Prosperity led the effort to remake a successful school diversity policy in Wake County, NC; which was the model

framework for scores of school districts across the country. The 2009 school board election provided the Koch brothers' front group an opportunity to lay the groundwork for candidates who advocate for re-segregation, or in Jim Crow terms "neighborhood schools."

- Cancer in Crossett – Koch Industries is among the top ten worst air polluters. And, Georgia Pacific, a Koch Industries subsidiary in Arkansas, is one of the largest manufacturers of the human carcinogen, formaldehyde. While the Koch brothers wage war against safety precautions, every day this factory is dumping millions of gallons of wastewater into streams that flow near a small rural town. The surrounding area is noticeably affected by air pollution – particularly in a minority neighborhood now dying of cancer. The brave community members of Crossett give powerful testimony to how they believe their health is being ravaged by a Koch Industries plant.
- Keystone XL – Koch Industries and its employees are the single largest oil and gas donors to the House Energy and Commerce Committee. Along with ample evidence linking the Kochs' business to the Canadian tar sands, they refuse to testify in Congress about their financial interest in the controversial Keystone XL. At the same time, the Kochs' allies in Congress are doing their best to stonewall and remove oversight.
- Higher Education – At a time when governments are slashing higher education funding, the Charles Koch Charitable Foundation has given more

than14.39 million in grants to over 150 universities. In return, some of these campuses are required to hire candidates who adhere to Koch-defined ideological guidelines.

During the 2010 mid term elections, the Koch brothers, alongside fellow billionaire Art Pope, funded a complete sweep of North Carolina's legislative and executive branches, which gave Republicans unilateral control of the state for the first time in more than 150 years. A remarkable political victory given the state voted for Obama in 2008, and that since the 1960s, North Carolina had been considered the most progressive of the old Confederacy, or as others have described it, "an oasis of moderation in the desert of reactionary politics." But thanks to the influx of corporate money, the radicals have transformed the state into an oasis of religious and pro-corporate extremism in the South's desert of religious and pro-corporate extremism. Dan Carter, professor at the University of South Carolina, assesses the current tumult in North Carolina and the hijacking of the state's political system, in a report titled 'North Carolina: A State of Shock. He writes:

> With a Republican governor and Republican controlled legislature, legislation enacted this year reads like a wish list ripped from the fulminations of Rush Limbaugh, Ralph Reed's right-wing Faith and Freedom Coalition and the editorial pages of the *Wall Street Journal*. For the gun lobby, there were new laws sealing public records that identified handgun permit holders while allowing those gun owners to carry their revolvers and semi-automatic pistols into restaurants, bars, parks, playgrounds, athletic

events, parades, funerals, and into the parking lots of public schools and universities.....here was also red meat for religious conservatives. During his 2012 campaign for governor, former Charlotte mayor Pat McCrory had promised to concentrate on promoting jobs while avoiding divisive issues like abortion. During the last days of the session, however, GOP leaders tacked a lengthy amendment onto an unrelated bill that mandated many hospital-level standards for the state's abortion clinics. If fully implemented, these requirements will leave only one North Carolina clinic in operation. Governor McCrory dutifully signed the measure.

But the payoff for the Koch brothers and the other corporate sponsors of the GOP program came in the form of a tax cut that the North Carolina Budget and Tax Center estimated would eventually cost one billion dollars per year with seventy five percent of the tax cut going to the top five percent of taxpayers.

You cannot discuss the Koch brothers without discussing the Tea Party. One of the great myths of American politics during the first term of Obama's presidency is that which concerns the Tea Party's self-proclaimed grassroots origins. The myth holds that the Tea Party was born when a CNBC reporter, Rick Santelli, launched into an on-air tirade against the Obama administration for backing a foreclosure relief bill. In his diatribe, he called for a "Chicago Tea Party." Following the Santelli outburst, the hash tag #TCOT (Top Conservatives on Twitter) went viral on twitter. Fox News ran the story and, by tax day on April 15, 2009, which was less than three months into Obama's presidency, Tea Parties had spread to nearly 1,000 communities throughout the country. Fox News was so swept up by the giddy anti-Obama rage that it was not uncommon to see the hosts of Fox & Friends joining in the cheering at Tea Party rallies. But what were they cheering for? No one seemed to know. If it started because of Santelli's rant against a modest foreclosure relief bill, then why was no one on the right protesting when President Bush bailed out the big banks with a trillion dollars relief package? In short, the Tea Party, of which less than 10 percent of its so-called members are not Caucasian, became a political movement that social conservatives and the Christian Right could hitch their wagon to.

In reality, the Tea Party's origins hold a far more sinister story. In fact, it's so far from being a grass roots movement that many commentators on the left have ridiculed it by labeling it an "astro-turf" movement. An astro-turf movement created by the Koch brothers and a number of companies that benefit most from anti-science voodoo (climate change deniers and tobacco companies), and those that benefit most from the elimination of taxes. A study funded by the National Cancer Institute of Health traces the roots of the Tea Party's anti-tax movement back to the 1980s when tobacco companies began to invest in third party groups to fight excise taxes on cigarettes, as well as muddying the waters when it came to linking cancer with passive smoking.

Stanton Glantz, a University of California, San Francisco (UCSF) professor of medicine, authored a report titled, *The Tobacco Industry and the Tea Party*. In it he writes: "Non-profit organizations associated with the Tea Party have longstanding ties to tobacco companies, and continue to advocate on behalf of the tobacco industry's anti-tax, anti-regulation agenda." The report identified two main organizations central to the Tea Party's emergence, *Americans for Prosperity* and *FreedomWorks*. "Both groups are now supporting the tobacco companies' political agenda by mobilizing local Tea Party opposition to tobacco taxes and smoke-free laws."

Moreover, FreedomWorks and Americans for Prosperity were once a single organization called Citizens for a Sound Economy (CSE). CSE was founded by the Koch brothers in the early 80s, and received more than $6 million from tobacco companies, including Philip Morris, between 1991 and 2004. Put that little factoid in your pipe and smoke it. But wait, there's more. In 1990, RJR Tobacco explained how groups like CSE were critical to the tobacco industry's fight against government regulation and excise taxes:

> ...coalition building should proceed along two tracks: a) a grassroots organizational and largely local track; b) and a national, intellectual track within the DC-New York corridor. Ultimately, we are talking about a "movement", a national effort to change the way people think about government's (and big business) role in our lives. Any such effort requires an intellectual foundation – a set of theoretical and ideological arguments on its behalf.

As you can see, the Tea Party movement is far from being the popular grassroots uprising that it pretends to be; it is, in fact, a quasi-movement guided by the velvet-gloved hand of big business and special interests. And the velvet glove is steered by the hand of Koch. Admit it, "Koch hands" sounds funny! What isn't funny, however, is where the hands of Koch went next – slipped under the gowns of the justices on the Supreme Court.

In 2007, Citizens for a Sound Economy rebranded and re-launched itself as Citizens United. In 2008, and with many on the far right fearing the then likelihood of a Hillary Clinton nomination and eventual presidency, the group produced an anti-Hillary documentary to be aired on cable during the 2008 Democratic primary. But due to the fact that Citizens United is an ideological group that takes for-profit corporate funding, the campaign finance laws prohibited this kind of "documentary" or advertisement to be aired in the period before an election. Citizens United argued against the corporate spending ban and in turn they took their case all the way to the Supreme Court.

Prior to Citizens United taking its case to the Supreme Court, however, corporations were already spending billions of dollars lobbying, and soliciting Political Action Committee (PAC) contributions. And Fortune 500 CEOs, whose wealth had grown exponentially compared to the wealth of their workers in recent decades, have always contributed robustly to candidates. But there was one crucial thing that the CEOs could not do: they could not siphon cash from their corporate war chests to bankroll campaigns for congressional or presidential candidates. This separation of corporations and candidates ensured corporations couldn't buy elections.

The Supreme Court heard the case of Citizens United and in a 5-4 decision that shocked even the most parochial right-wing nuts, the Roberts Court ruled not only in favor of the Koch Brother's non-profit group, but bulldozed the foundational understanding of the corporation that had governed American law for more than 200 years.

In one foul swoop, the court obliterated every finance law that had been put in place to safeguard our democracy, from Roosevelt's efforts in 1907 through to the bipartisan McCain-Feingold Campaign Finance Reform Act of 2002. Bang! Gone! Effectively, the Supreme Court decision allows corporations free reign to inject as much money as they please into federal campaigns. *Slate*'s Dahlia Lithwich calls it "The Pinocchio Project," in which the Court transforms "a corporation into a real live boy," complete with personhood, free speech rights and "the unfettered opportunity to drown the body politic in a tidal wave of pervasive incentives."

President Obama described the Court's decision thus:

> With its ruling today, the Supreme Court has given a green light to a new stampede of special interest money in our politics. It is a major victory for big oil, Wall Street banks, health insurance companies, and the other powerful interests that marshal their power every day in Washington to drown out the voices of everyday Americans.

Without surprise, the proxy party of corporate interests, the GOP, holds a diametrically opposite view to Obama. In fact, they've doubled down on this catastrophic Supreme Court ruling, and have plans to strike down the Tillman Act of 1907. The Republican National Committee (RNC) filed an amicus brief with the Fourth Circuit Court of Appeals. The brief states that the Tillman Act "artificially disadvantages political party and candidate committees by forcing them to rely on aggregating small donations from individuals while allowing other political actors, such as independent-expenditure-only political action committees, to receive unlimited corporate donations."

This is a despicably ballsy attempt to inject even more corporate cash into the political process. Marge Baker, executive vice president of the liberal group People for the American Way, wrote, "It's remarkable that the Republican Party is publicly taking the position that there's not enough corporate money in politics. It's amazing!" If the RNC wins this value add on and the Tillman Act becomes another corporate road kill, corporations will still be bound to the same donor limits as flesh-and-blood people. But unlike people, corporations can be easily created in order to exceed those limits.

In short, the ruling means there are now no checks on the ability of corporations or other giant aggregators of power to decide our elections. None! It means corporations can spend all the money they want and, sooner rather than later, they will plant in every office in every district, state, and executive office the plant of their choice. It means every congressman, senator, governor and president will be held accountable, not to their respective constituents, but to the boardrooms of big business. It's impossible to overstate how great a blow this ruling is to our democracy. It's nothing less than a political science nightmare. It now creates a scenario where private citizens, like you and me, are irrelevant in the campaign funding process. It means critics can now be silenced and bought off. It flies in the face of free speech. It means money equals free speech. It means the next nine judges on the Supreme Court will be appointed by presidents who were appointed by corporations. It is government of the people by the corporations for the corporations.

On the day of the Court's decision, former MSNBC anchor Keith Olbermann gave the following warnings:

- Be prepared for laws that eliminate or neuter unions
- Be prepared for a reduction of taxes for the wealthy and corporations
- Be prepared for the elimination of social safety nets, because money spent on the poor means less money in the pool for the corporations
- Be prepared for wars sold as new products. Think Halliburton and Blackwater
- Be prepared for bans on abortion, same sex marriage, evolution being taught, and the separation of Church and State.
- Be prepared for racial and religious profiling because you have to blame somebody for all the reductions in spending and civil liberties to make sure the agitators against the Corporate United States of America remain unheard
- Be prepared for bank reforms to be rolled back. Reforms that were put in place to prevent another global meltdown like that of 2007
- Be prepared for Walmart candidates for local towns sponsored by Walmart
- Be prepared for a Sarah Palin presidency
- Be prepared for the end of independent news agencies
- Be prepared for Rupert Murdoch to buy the Associated Press

Shortly after the Citizens United v Federal Election Commission ruling on January 21, 2010, came the mid-term elections. With the door effectively kicked open to unlimited corporate money, Republican affiliated organizations poured more than $500 million into 2010 congressional races. The results of these races gave America a glimpse into its future, a future besieged by crackpot crazies.

Typically, off-year elections favor Republicans, as seniors and evangelicals are the only reliable demographic that turns out to vote. But with the Democrats winning so decisively in 2008, that should have been enough of a buffer to deal with even the wildest of swings to the Republicans. But super PACs like American Crossroads, which was founded by Karl Rove (the architect for driving evangelicals to the polls in 2000 and 2004) and former RNC Chairman Ed Gillespie, pumped millions of dollars into every congressional race that was within reach. In fact, Gillespie helped pump more than $40 million into key state legislative races in 2010 with the intention of bolstering Republicans who could gerrymander new GOP congressional districts. We will talk more about gerrymandering in later chapters, but Gillespie told donors that investing $5 million in 2010 was the equivalent of $25 million in 2012, in terms of electing Republicans and changing the nation's electoral map.

"Dark money" flowed through to Republican campaigns via C-4 groups. C-4 is short for section 501(c)4 of the tax code. These groups are identified by the IRS as non-profit "social welfare" groups, but instead have been hijacked by the likes of Rove, Gillespie and others to launder the flow of contributions, so that corporations can retain their anonymity.

In 2012, the IRS finally caught wind of the fact that these C-4s were being used as anything but a social welfare group and they went ahead and audited a number of them. Yes, that's the big IRS scandal. The scandal is the IRS did their fucking job – i.e. asked questions to investigate whether or not there was any wrongdoing.

So what did all this dark money bring to our democracy? It opened up the asylum to the lunatics. More than 87 congressional seats transferred from Democrats to Republicans. Seven senate seats did the same, as did eight governorships.

Let's look at some of the best quotables from the 2010 freshman class of crazies:

Sen. Ted Cruz (R-Texas): "We need 100 more like Jesse Helms in the Senate." (NB: Sen. Jesse Helms was a white supremacist, Klan advocate, and who once said, "Every case of AIDS can be traced to homosexuality sodomy.")

Jeff Duncan (South Carolina -03): "There are genuine questions to be asked about the validity of Obama's presidency, his phony identification papers, and whether in fact he was born in Kenya." Duncan now serves as Chairman on the House Homeland Security Oversight Committee.

Allen West (Florida –22): "Every time I see one of those 'Coexist' bumper stickers, I look at the person inside that is driving. Because that person represents something that would give away our country. Would give away who we are, our rights and freedoms and liberties because they are afraid to stand up and confront that which is the antithesis, anathema of who we are." If you think that was pleasant, here's what West had to say about gender equality, "Liberal women have been neutering American men and bringing us to the point of this incredible weakness – to let them know that we are not going to have our men become subservient."

Nikki Haley (South Carolina Governor): "Raped and battered women are distractions that represent a small portion of South Carolina's population" is what she said in justifying her decision to veto critical funding that goes to programs that work to prevent domestic abuse and rape.

Rand Paul (Kentucky): "I'm not a firm believer in democracy." There's enough material to write an entire book on Rand Paul alone, and it's likely he will be a serious challenger for the GOP nomination for 2016, but here's something that should make you really concerned about what's in the mind of this extremely religious, severely conservative crackpot. In 2010, Paul's stance on civil rights came under scrutiny when he had difficulty answering whether or not he would have voted for the Civil Rights Act of 1964 in an interview with the *Louisville Courier Journal*'s editorial board: "I like the Civil Rights Act in the sense that it ended discrimination in all public domains, and I'm all in favor of that. I don't like the idea of telling private business owner – I abhor racism. I think it's a bad business decision to exclude anybody from your restaurant – but, at the same time, I do believe in private ownership. But I absolutely think there should be no discrimination in anything that gets any public funding, and that's most of what I think the Civil Rights Act was about in my mind."

Bam right there – in Paul's mind, private ownership supersedes everything in his god fearing, corporate fellating persona, including civil rights. And we need only Google some of the more quotable remarks from other Tea Party caucus members such as Michele Bachmann, and Todd Akin. You see, their corporate sponsors don't care what self-righteous, religious rationalizations spew forth from the mouths of these lunatics, so long as these elected religious zealots continue to chant the mantra, "Cut taxes for the wealthy, and cut regulations for corporations." While these Tea Party crazies protest mosques at Ground Zero or declare there are "Muslims secretly embedded in the Oval Office", their corporate sponsors continue to bring great harm to America while simultaneously bringing great benefits to the plutocratic elite. Case in point, the negotiations over the debt ceiling. Not only do polls show that a majority of Tea Party Republicans fail to comprehend the difference between the national debt and budget deficits, but their intransigence on striking any deal that would account for a balance between spending cuts and tax increases on the wealthy threatened the nation with defaulting on its commitments for the first time in its history. The debacle prompted Standard and Poor to issue a credit downgrade for the United States. The original report from S&P made it quite clear that it was the "no tax increases on the wealthy no matter what" position of the Tea Party and other far right Republicans that precipitated their decision to issue the downgrade.

It's no secret that the Tea Party and its 2010 freshman class of congressmen have a weak grasp of public policy issues, and a poor comprehension of books that lack centerfolds. The Right's orchestrated campaign of misinformation was designed to ensure their base would fail to comprehend the facts of the debate – that lifting the debt ceiling did not grant Obama the right to spend more money, it merely meant America could honor its commitment to debts already accrued. What the Right also didn't explain to its voters was that a default and downgrade means higher interest rates, which further damages confidence in the still fragile economy, which leads to reduced further investments. But the party of anti-science and anti-math held the economy to ransom and publicly threatened default, regardless of cost.

Without specifically mentioning Republicans, S&P senior director Joydeep Mukherji said the stability and effectiveness of American political institutions were undermined by the fact that "people in the political arena were even talking about a potential default. That a country even has such voices, albeit a minority, is something notable. This kind of rhetoric is not common amongst AAA sovereigns."

What the S&P director is saying here is straightforward: if the government (congress) of a nation publicly questions whether its debts should be paid, then it stands to reason that investors should be more cautious about presuming whether or not those debts will be repaid. If politicians voice that debts should be held hostage until political favors are offered in return, then by definition those debts are less safe than they were before. In simpler terms, threatening the integrity of U.S. credit has the direct result of, well, threatening the integrity of U.S. credit. It's for this very reason that far right talk of taking the economy hostage was deemed equally dangerous and vile by the world's leading credit agency.

Chuck Hagel, the former Republican Senator from Nebraska and current Defense Secretary, called his party "irresponsible" and said he was "disgusted" by the antics of his fellow Republicans over the debt ceiling:

> The irresponsible actions of my party, the Republican Party over this were astounding. I'd never seen anything like this in my lifetime....I was very disappointed. I was very disgusted in how this played out in Washington, this debt ceiling debate. It was

an astounding lack of responsible leadership by many in the Republican Party, and I say that as a Republican....I think the Republican Party is captive to political movements that are very ideological, that are very narrow. I've never seen so much intolerance as I see today.

Mike Lofgren, a veteran Republican congressional staffer, wrote an essay on why he ended his career on the Hill after nearly thirty years:

It should have been evident to clear-eyed observers that the Republican Party is becoming less and less like a traditional political party in a representative democracy and becoming more like an apocalyptic cult, or one of the intensely ideological authoritarian parties of 20th century Europe.

Hostage taking, ultimatums, walkouts and tantrums are now the hallmark of the Tea Party and the Christian Right. In days past, freshmen would enter congress as "newbies" or "bed wetters." Speakers would advise their new caucus members that the way to get along is to go along. In other words, keep your head down, learn the ropes, and build alliances and partnerships. But that 200-year advice wasn't good enough for this bunch of nihilists, who seem more intent on burning the House down rather than climbing up its stairs. Republican congressman Joe Walsh said, "I came here ready to go to war. The political powers will always try to get you to compromise your beliefs for the good of the team. The people didn't send me here to compromise."

Compromise has always been a holy word in Washington. Compromise is how the chambers of American political power have brokered the nation's most significant achievements. It's how we've passed laws. It's how we've avoided the bloodshed of another civil war. But for the Christian Right, compromise is viewed on par with doing a deal with the Devil. In a speech given in April 2012, President Obama said, "The challenge we have right now is that we have one side, a party that will brook no compromise. The Republican's radical vision is antithetical to our entire history as a land of opportunity." The editor of the *New York Times* hailed the President's remarks: "In this speech, he (Obama) finally conceded that the Republican Party has demonstrated no interest in the values of compromise and realism."

That this country has successfully met so many challenges and crises in its tumultuous history is due largely to an effective government, and an effective government is dependent on a loyal opposition. Loyalty to the country has always superseded loyalty to one's party. But not now! This right wing intransigence is an understated threat to the welfare of its citizens, and it's not just partisan left wing foot soldiers making this claim, for even the former Australian treasurer Wayne Swan, whose country avoided recession during the global financial crisis, commented on the debt ceiling debate debacle: "Let's be blunt and acknowledge the biggest threat to the world's biggest economy are the cranks and crazies that have taken over the Republican Party. Despite President Obama's goodwill and strong efforts, the national interest was held hostage by the rise of the extreme Tea Party wing of the Republican Party."

In the 18th century, Edmund Burke, who is widely viewed as the philosophical founder of modern conservatism, wrote, "All government, indeed every human benefit and enjoyment, every virtue, and every prudent act, is founded on compromise and barter." The Founding Fathers placed compromise at the heart of the Constitution – compromise between the federal and state governments, between the branches of government, and even between the two houses of Congress. America has always been a grand experiment in compromise.

Fast-forward to mid-2013 and again the GOP's unwillingness to compromise threatens to shut down the federal government. The far right refuses to entertain any budget that includes funding for the Affordable Health Act. Tea Party fuck, and a likely 2014 presidential front-runner, Senator Marco Rubio, said, "If you pay for a budget that pays for ObamaCare, you have voted for ObamaCare." Notwithstanding the fact that House Republicans have voted to repeal ObamaCare no less than 40 times and have failed. Notwithstanding the fact it's the law. To ignore a law that was passed democratically is in itself undemocratic. In fact, given that the extreme levels of opposition and obstruction are being conducted with the implicit purpose and intent to undermine the nation's economic recovery, does this not constitute sedition at the least, if not treason at the very worst?

This is who apathetic progressives opened the door to in 2010. This is who big corporations sponsored into office thanks to the Supreme Court's "money equals free speech" verdict. The Christian Right are now governing and, with more dark money flowing into future political races, the Christian Right could end up buying all three branches of government. If that happens, prepare yourself for a new feudalism, where the citizenry would be reduced to peasantry, paying rents and taxes to corporate overlords and tithes to government-established religious organizations.

For our elected officials, the Supreme Court's decision means politicians now spend all their time raising money and campaigning, which leaves them little or no time to do what it is they were sent to Washington to do: to fix America's problems.

CHAPTER THREE
RIGGING THE GAME (PART 1)

"She was from the wrong side of the tracks no matter how you gerrymandered the town."

JAMES LILEKS FALLING UP THE STAIRS

Unlimited corporate money and the support of the Christian Right swept the crazies on the far right into state legislatures, governor houses and Congress in 2010. In fact, the Republican Party had a net gain of more than 690 state legislature seats. This election held added strategic advantage for the Right as 2010 was a census year, which presented the respective victors of state legislatures with a once in a decade opportunity to redraw congressional maps. This election gave Republicans majorities in the state houses, which allowed them a once in a decade opportunity to redistrict themselves into districts that would outperform the party in future elections, had the districts not changed. Effectively, redistricting (gerrymandering) is a deceitful tactic to change the political geography of a state to your electoral advantage. Redistricting has allowed Republicans to turn once blue states into right wing laboratories. Overturning and destroying things that took decades to build. Now we're stuck with an uneven playing field until at least the next census year of 2020, and beyond if "we" don't do something about it.

Their strategy of redistricting or gerrymandering is no secret, surprisingly. You would think any political plan that attempts to subvert democracy would be hacked together in the basement of Karl Rove's mansion, with the details leaked only to the closest of party insiders. But no, the blueprint for keeping control of national and state legislatures, even in the face of majority opposition, is plainly spelled out for all to see. On the GOP-sponsored website RedistrictingMajorityProject.com, you will find the following:

> Every 10 years a census is taken, and congressional districts are redrawn. This process is known as "redistricting," and is one of the most important processes of our democracy. Election Day 2010 proved to be an even bigger "wave" election at the state level than anticipated. Republicans flipped at least 19 legislative bodies to Republican control and hold majorities in 10 of the 15 states that will gain or lose U.S. House seats and where the legislature plays a role in redrawing the map.
>
> Republicans have an opportunity to create 20-25 new Republican Congressional Districts through the redistricting process over the next five election cycles, solidifying a Republican House majority.

The Republican State Legislative Committee (RSLC) is the chief sponsor of the Redistricting Majority Project. As it is organized as a type of political group, it can take in unlimited corporate donations. Along with Wal-Mart and tobacco companies, the RSLC's largest funders in 2010 were the Chamber of Commerce and American Justice Partnership, whom gave a combined $6.5 million.

After stunning losses in the 2008 election, the Republican Party made re-districting its priority. In 2010, Karl Rove explained, "Some of the most important contests this Fall will be way down the ballot in state legislative races that will determine who redraws congressional district lines after this year's census, a process that could determine which party controls upwards of 20 seats and whether many other seats will be competitive."

You see, demographically, the Right is running out of angry, retired white voters. And in the words of Stephen Colbert, "It only looks bleaker for Republicans in the future. Unless science can find a way for Latino women to give birth to old white men." Given the great difficulty of implementing Colbert's mock hypothetical, the GOP is left with the dilemma of having to water down their radical political message ("Rape is so misunderstood") in an effort to win over more voters, or taking the Lance Armstrong route of cheating to win. Predictably, they chose the latter path: the path of gerrymandering, and voter suppression. And it's paying dividends in a big way for them. In the 2012 general election, the GOP lost the popular vote by five million votes, but kept control of the House by a 33-seat margin. So much for that cutesy idealism, the will of the people!

In fact, a million more Americans voted for Democrats seeking election to the U.S. House of Representatives than Republicans. But that popular vote advantage did not result in control of the chamber for the Democrats. Instead, despite getting fewer votes, Republicans have a commanding control of the House. This should alarm you! These Republican rule changes are a major blow to democracy, as we know it. By design, redistricting eliminates the competition and virtually guarantees the incumbent maintains power. In a healthy democracy, voters choose their representatives. With redistricting, it becomes the other way around.

Republican strategist Karl Rove bragged, "He who controls redistricting controls Congress." This approach paid off. In 2010 state races, Republicans picked up 675 legislative seats, gaining complete control of 12 state legislatures. As a result, the GOP oversaw redrawing of lines for four times as many congressional districts as Democrats. The RedMap project was so successful for the GOP that it also increased its share of House and Senate seats by almost 10 percent, from approximately 3200 to 3900. It took control of both the legislative chambers in 25 states and won total control of 21 states (legislature and governorship). In 17 of these states, GOP legislatures controlled the redistricting for 173 seats.

So how does redistricting work? First you need to redraw district maps, which can be expensive. To redesign maps to your advantage, one needs a lot of extensive data, sophisticated software and skillful map drawers. Here's where all that corporate money comes to the fore. Flush with this dark money, the RSLC were able to hire teams of technical experts to draw voting districts that look visually like the most absurd shapes you could ever imagine. Reshaped districts have the map appearance of a double-ended hammer, sea monkeys, or an egg on a toothpick. The reason for these visually odd shapes is that the key part of the redistricting strategy is to push minority voters into fewer reliable left-leaning districts, in a process that is commonly known as "packing".

Packing is to concentrate as many voters of one type into a single electoral district to minimize their influence in other districts. Another part of the strategy is what's known as "cracking," which involves spreading voters of a particular type among many districts in order to deny them a sufficiently large voting bloc in any particular district. An example of this would be to split the voters in a reliably Democratic district among several districts where the majority of voters are Republican. Ultimately, the two goals of redistricting are to maximize the effect of supporters' votes, and to minimize the effect of opponents' votes.

Imagine a hypothetical Republican-controlled state that has five congressional seats and only 20 voters in each. That makes 100 voters in total. Let's say 55 are Republicans, and 45 are Democrats. In this instance, a representative proportion of seats would be three Republican representatives and two Democrats. Now imagine you can redraw the district boundaries any way you wish. The only condition is you must keep 20 voters in each. The Republican Party would carve up the state so that there were 11 Republicans and nine Democrats in each of the five districts. In this instance, the GOP would win the congressional seats of this hypothetical state 5 to 0, while holding only a narrow popular vote margin. This is a distortion of the democratic process.

To further demonstrate using a real life example: The RSLC strategy in North Carolina was to push minority voters into three districts. In two of those districts, African-American incumbents had been holding office for years. The RLSC redrew maps that added yet more African-Americans to these two districts. Tom Hofeller, the RSLC-appointed architect of Republican-friendly maps going back decades, wrote in an email about one of the districts, "The plan was to incorporate all the significant concentrations of minority voters in the northeast into the first district." A third district was 120-mile long, shaped like a hammer, connecting pockets of black voters from three different distant cities. The maps were designed to "segregate African-American voters in three districts and concede those districts to the Democrats," says Bob Hall of Democracy North Carolina, a nonpartisan public interest group that joined the lawsuit against the new maps.

The result? The redrawn maps worked perfectly in favor of the GOP in 2012. Democratic candidates for the House won 50.6 percent of the total vote in the state of North Carolina, but that translated into just four Democrats taking office in the state's House, compared to the nine Republicans who did same. In other words, for the Democrats, a greater than 50 percent popular vote translated into holding less than 33 percent of the legislative representation. In the months following Mitt Romney's heavy loss to President Obama, the RSLC boasted:

> Pennsylvanians cast 83,000 more votes for Democratic U.S. House candidates than their Republican opponents, but elected a 13-5 Republican majority to represent them in Washington; Michiganders cast over 240,000 more votes for Democratic congressional candidates than Republicans, but still elected a 9-5 Republican delegation to Congress. Nationwide, Republicans won 54 percent of the U.S. House seats, along with 58 of 99 state legislative chambers, while winning only 8 of 33 U.S. Senate races and carrying only 47.8 percent of the national presidential vote.

All in all, the GOP lost the House popular vote by more than 1.3 million votes, but this translated into a loss of just eight congressional seats. To further underscore what such a sabotage of democracy looks like, consider some of the following striking examples:

North Carolina: In 2010, the House delegation was 7 to 6 in favor of Democrats. In 2012, the Democrats won 50.1 percent of congressional votes, but the new redistricting laws gave the GOP a 9 to 4 congressional majority.

Michigan: In 2012, Democrats won more than 54 percent of the vote in state House elections but netted only 46 percent of the seats.

Ohio: In 2012, Democrats won 51 percent of the state House vote, but Democrats received only 43 of the 99 seats.

North Carolina: In 2012, Republicans narrowly edged out Democrats with 51 percent of the state House vote but ended up with more than double the number of seats – 34 to 16.

Herman Schwartz, a constitutional law professor at the American University Washington College of Law, writes:

> The post-2010 Southern gerrymandering virtually guarantees that all the Southern legislatures will remain Republican for the foreseeable future, regardless of the popular vote. This, together with the GOP's congressional gerrymandering elsewhere in the country, will produce a substantial ultra-conservative block in the U.S. Congress and is almost certain to make it extremely difficult for the Democrats to retake the House. Even if the Democrats take the presidency and the Senate, the result is likely to be a continuation of what we have today: gridlock and a failure to deal with the pressing problems we face.

But that's the evil genius of redistricting: instead of voters getting to pick their leaders, leaders get to pick their voters. In other words, "Me, the people!" Now that the GOP has mastered redistricting at the state level, they are moving forward to take it to the next level. In other words, putting a lock on the presidency without the will of the majority. The Republican Party is not only moving to scrap the entire electoral college system, despite it being to their advantage in Bush winning without the popular vote in 2000; Republican legislators in the key swing states of Michigan, Pennsylvania, Ohio, Wisconsin, and Virginia, are moving behind proposals that would allocate presidential electoral college votes by congressional district. Pennsylvania state senator Dominic Pilleggi (R) argues, "The current winner-takes-all system is inherently unfair because the losing party gets no credit in the electoral count." Yes, exactly! Since when does the losing party get to pick the President? But the GOP plan flips that notion on its head: if electoral votes were allocated by congressional districts in the 2012 general election, as the GOP hopes to do in the future, then Mitt Romney would have won the presidency, despite polling 5 million fewer votes than Obama.

Herman Schwartz warns,

> Unless the Democrats wake up to the importance of winning state legislative elections, they are likely to remain a largely impotent minority in the House of Representatives and equally feeble in the state legislatures. The momentous Supreme Court decisions on the Voting Rights Act, same-sex marriage and affirmative action make winning these races all the more vital, for all these rulings deal with state action. The huge Republican victory in the 2010 election could turn out to be a gift that keeps giving.

What does that mean for us atheists? Well, it means free reign for the radicals to enact their religious 17th century agenda. By turning so many congressional districts "ruby red", the Republican Party is forced to move further and further to the extreme right, all but ensuring the Christian Right drives the GOP agenda. With so many seats now made artificially safe by gerrymandering, Republican incumbents need not fear being defeated by a Democrat in coming elections for the foreseeable future. Who they risk being defeated by, however, is an opponent within their own party. Bearing in mind the Republican base consists largely of social conservatives, so-called "moderate Republicans" are being ousted by extremists during the primary process. Today, the greatest fear of nearly every Republican incumbent is to be "primaried" by a party colleague, which has the end result of pulling the entire party farther to the right. This is leading the Republican Party to become increasingly more isolated from the will of America. Poll after poll shows a majority of Americans favor liberal policies, from gun control to women's rights; from tax policies that demand the wealthy pay a greater share to attitudes towards same-sex marriage. But our representatives in state and federal legislatures are writing laws contrary to popular American attitudes. For Republican incumbents, there is only one demographic on the American electoral landscape that counts: the white Christian Right.

CHAPTER FOUR
FIXING THE GAME (PART 2)

"If voter ID fraud is so widespread, how come it's invisible?"

COLIN POWELL

The changing demographics of America means the Republican Party and their corporate sponsors are unable to depend solely on angry white Christians to carry the load on Election Day. This demographic hurdle is becoming increasingly higher for conservatives to clear, and thus they're becoming increasingly desperate in their attempts to retain power. And what do people do when they're desperate to win? Well, they invariably cheat! And no one cheats better than the super wealthy! Don't believe me? If you want to find the biggest asshole in the room, play a game of Monopoly.

But the GOP had a problem going into the 2012 election. "Many Americans saw voting both as a right and a rite, a core value and an almost sacred tradition. "So Republicans needed a cover story," writes Jonathan Alter. The cover story they chose is to perpetuate what has been wholly discredited as a complete fabrication – that massive and widespread voter fraud threatens the integrity of the ballot box.

Republican National Committee Chairman Reince Pribus, which is my favorite Latin word for the taint, declared that Wisconsin is "absolutely riddled with voter fraud." In fact, the state's voter fraud rate in 2004 was 0.0002 percent – just seven votes.

In 2008, John McCain said fraudulent registrations collected by ACORN were "one of the greatest frauds in voter history in this country, maybe destroying the fabric of democracy." The Congressional Research Service, however, found no proof that anyone improperly registered by ACORN tried to vote improperly.

While defending its precedent-setting photo ID law before the Supreme Court, Indiana was unable to cite a single instance of voter impersonation in its entire history. But if you had have tuned into Fox News on any given day during the 2012 campaign, you would have found at least one hour of each 12-hour cycle dedicated to covering alleged stories of voter fraud. Stories that, ultimately, led nowhere, despite the sense of onscreen hysteria that led to Republican Governor of South Carolina claiming "dead zombies" had voted in the 2012 election. Highlighting a report from DMV Director and a Hayley appointee, Kevin Shwedo, the Governor claimed a review of the state records had determined around 950 dead people might have voted in the 2010 election. Looks like someone thought *World War Z* was a documentary. While Shwedo admitted that reporting errors could have led to the discrepancy, the GOP suggested that the identities had been assumed with the purpose to commit voter fraud, and thus this was the basis for justifying the enactment of controversial voter ID laws in the state.

In July of 2013, a report proved Governor Hayley's claim to be bogus. South Carolina House Democratic Leader Todd Rutherford accused Hayley and other Republicans of deliberately and deceptively pushing false claims for political gain. Now we have the proof that shows that the accusations of voter fraud were completely without merit," said Rutherford. "And once again, South Carolina's taxpayers have to foot the bill for the millions of dollars unnecessarily spent as a result of Governor Haley and her colleagues' incompetence and blind-ideology." Rutherford went on to call for Hayley to "acknowledge that they were being dishonest about voter fraud" and to "apologize to the public." On July 9, 2013, Hayley did exactly that, to her credit.

Voter ID fraud is so rare, in fact, that you're more likely to sight a UFO than to find an actual incidence of a voter using a fake ID, stealing an identity, or voting twice. Not only are the penalties huge – carrying up to five years imprisonment – but what does the individual committing the voter fraud stand to gain by voting illegally? Extrapolate that further – why would an undocumented worker, for example, which the Republicans most fear to be committing voter fraud, go to the hassle of obtaining a fake social security number, only to step forth from the shadows to cast a vote on election day, with the risk of being caught and deported forever?

The total number of federal convictions for election fraud in the years 2002-05 amounts to:

- Voting while ineligible: 18
- Voting multiple times: 5
- Registration fraud: 3

In all, the above numbers are not enough to swing a Bakersfield Rotary Club election for a raffle ticket secretary.

But facts never deter Republicans from indulging in erroneous fear-mongering if it means advancing their agenda. Their agenda being to keep minorities, who typically lean left during elections, from casting ballots at the polls. Conservative columnist John Fund declared on Fox

News that, "To deny that voter fraud isn't going on is to frankly deny reality." Further amusing is the fact Fund said this the day after a study found just 10 verifiable instances of in-person voter fraud that voter ID laws have been intended to prevent since 2000. In August of 2012, the *Washington Post* reported that any type of in-person voter fraud is exceedingly rare. After examining the results of 2,068 reports of election fraud, fewer than 10 instances were found where an individual impersonated another person in order to cast a ballot.

Lorraine C. Minnite, author of *The Myth of Voter Fraud*, writes, "Voter fraud is a politically constructed myth…Voter fraud politics are robust in part because they capitalize on general and widely held folk beliefs that are rooted in facts and actual experience, notions such as corruption in party politics and government but also stereotypes and class and racially biased preconceptions of corruption among groups long stigmatized by their marginal or minority status in U.S. society."

Katrina vanden Heuval, in a *Washington Post* op-ed, paints a disturbing picture of Republican voter suppression in a number of state legislatures:

> In states across the country, Republican legislatures are pushing through laws that make it more difficult for Americans to vote. The most popular include new laws requiring voters to bring official identification to the polls. Estimates suggest that more than one in 10 Americans lack an eligible form of ID, and thus would be turned away at their polling location. Most are minorities and young people, the most loyal constituencies of the Democratic Party…Voter fraud, in truth, is essentially nonexistent.

A report from the Brennan Center for Justice found the incidence of voter fraud at rates such as 0.0003 percent in Missouri and 0.000009 percent in New York. "Voter impersonation is an illusion," said Michael Waldman, executive director of the Brennan Center. "It almost never happens, and when it does, it is in numbers far too small to effect the outcome of even a close election."

In a 2010 poll of Republicans, 21 percent of respondents believed that a non-partisan activist organization called ACORN, whose focus is advocacy for low-income Americans, stole the 2008 election for Obama. 55 percent of respondents said they were unsure. Leaving less than 25 percent who rejected this absurdity outright. Apparently, ACORN's first "mistake" was to endorse then candidate Obama for the presidency. It's second mistake was to volunteer in helping new voter registration drives, and on this, ACORN paid its foot soldiers on a per signature basis, which is the very same way most activist organizations pay theirs. But people being people, a small number of ACORN workers saw an opportunity to defraud their employer by claiming new registered voters who weren't in fact real people, for the exclusive motive of boosting their result-based salary. Thus, when ACORN looked closely at some of the signatures, they saw names like "Mickey Mouse", "Donald Duck", and "Yosemite Sam." But, obviously, there was never any likelihood of a Donald Duck from Columbus, Ohio, coming out to vote on Election Day. Thus, the victim here was exclusively ACORN, and the damage they suffered was in over-paying a handful of their workers. Ultimately, this was nothing more than registration fraud. But this didn't stop the right wing talking heads whipping their supporters into a frenzy over

ACORN and the falsehood that ACORN is a left wing group that facilitates voter ID fraud.

If you want to know how far the Right's false outrage is based from reality, consider that in March of 2013, House Republicans approved a measure blocking funding for ACORN, despite the fact that non-existent organizations are not in the business of seeking funds. In other words, ACORN permanently closed its doors in 2010.

Suppressing the vote is hardly a new dynamic on the American political landscape. In the early 20th century, Southern Democrats imposed literacy tests, "grandfather clauses" (voters were barred from casting a ballot if their grandfathers hadn't, which was impossible to prove for blacks), and poll taxes designed to disenfranchise minorities. Many Americans are old enough to remember Jim Crow-era laws. Republicans, yes, the party of Abraham Lincoln, first took up voter suppression tactics in the aftermath of the 1960 election of President Kennedy, when they accused the then Chicago Mayor of stealing votes for the Democrats in the river wards of Chicago. In 1964, the RNC launched "Operation Eagle Eye" under the guise of guarding against voter fraud, but it was nothing more than a ruse to scare African-American voters away from the polling booths.

The only large-scale, verifiable case of voter fraud that's ever been discovered in the US of A was discovered in the Supreme Court aftermath of the 2000 election Gore v Bush. The conservative-dominated Court ruled a shutdown of the Florida recount, which handed victory to the candidate who often hurts himself chasing a balloon in a park. What followed was years of investigations and recounts, with Democrats convinced the Republicans had stolen the race for Bush. In 2004, a full four years after the election, Democrat fears were vindicated when it turned out that the Republican legislature in Florida had purged more than fifty thousand voters from voter polls on the basis they were ex-convicts. As it turned out, fewer than 30 percent of these lists were accurate. In other words, thirty-thousand voters, an overwhelming number of whom were Democrats and more than 50 percent of whom were black, in a state where 15 percent are African-American, were unlawfully barred from casting a vote. In an election that came down to just a couple of hundred votes, this made all the difference. A difference all right! For it resulted in a Bush presidency, which led to an unjustifiable war in Iraq, a collapsed economy, and the appointment of two radical conservatives to the Supreme Court bench.

What did I say about elections having consequences?

In returning to the fact that the Republican Party committed the only case of widespread voter fraud in recent memory, isn't it amazing how they've spun the debate to dress themselves as the victim?

By painting themselves as the victims, the Republican Party has successfully used that cover fire with their constituents as justification for enacting unapologetic voter suppression laws. Voter suppression is a strategy to influence the outcome of an election by discouraging or preventing people from exercising their right to vote. The tactics of voter suppression can range from dirty tricks or law changes that make voting inconvenient, through to blatantly illegal activities that physically intimidate prospective voters from casting a ballot.

Let's get one thing straight: 100 percent of all voter suppression tactics deployed in this country are being carried out by the Republican Party or Republican groups, whereas the Democrats are doing the complete opposite. In fact, it was Democrats that passed the Motor Voter ID Act in 1993. The intention of the legislation was to encourage greater access to voter registration for the citizens who needed further assistance registering to vote. In other words, voters could register to vote at their respective DMV. The Democratic Party also have get out the vote programs like Rock the Vote and Souls to the Polls, while the GOP has Assholes Blocking the Polls. It's impossible not to see how far apart the two major political parties are on this critical component of our democracy.

In state after state, in race after race, Republicans are distributing pamphlets that include incorrect election dates; hiding ballot boxes; using voting machines that don't work; challenging voters as they show up. In fact, the Brennan Center for Justice New York tabled a list of voter suppression tactics the Republican Party was actively engaging in:

1. **Changing polling locations.** An election official can do this as close as the day prior to the election.

2. **Changing polling hours or eliminating early voting days.** This can be particularly problematic in urban areas where long polling lines are most likely. Why should voters have to wait two hours in line to vote in America, the greatest democracy in the world?

3. **Reducing the number of polling places.** This raises the same problem as above, particularly when the eliminated polling places had disproportionately served minority communities.

4. **At-large elections.** At-large elections for school-board members or city councils often dilute the voting power of minorities who have greater influence in single-candidate district elections. In an at-large election, a cohesive voting block with 51 percent of the vote can elect 100 percent of the officials.

5. **Packing majority-minority districts.** Election maps drawn to push all of a community's minorities in one or a handful of districts can dilute their respective voting power.

6. **Dividing minority districts.** Similarly, election maps can slice minority communities into multiple districts so that they have no cumulative influence in any one place. The line between these two tactics is a fine one (and also illustrates why the VRA was useful for assessing facts on the ground).

7. **Voter ID laws:** This increasingly popular tactic, sometimes likened to a modern-day poll tax, has the potential to disenfranchise voters who don't have a driver's license, or who don't have the money or ability to obtain one (a disproportionate share of these people are minorities). Such laws can also have a disproportionate impact in cities, where many people don't own cars.

8. **Onerous candidate qualifications.** For example, voters must be landowners to be eligible to vote.

9. **Changing multi-lingual voter assistance.** Making it harder for non-English language speakers to vote.

10. **Changing election dates**. Confusion reduces voter turnout.

11. **Creating** *new* **elections.** Confusion reduces voter turnout.

12. **Canceling elections.** Confusion reduces voter turnout.

Moreover, Republicans have been so successful in perpetuating the myth of voter ID fraud via their media arm, Fox News, that opinion polls show overwhelming public support for "tightening" voter laws. Winning the spin, therefore, has provided the additional cover fire to enact voter suppression laws through state legislatures. In the battleground state of Pennsylvania, for example, the Republican controlled legislature passed a voting law in early 2012 that required all voters to have a "valid"' photo ID. By valid, I mean valid in the eyes of *this* law. For example, the law requires a photo ID to have an expiry date, thus ruling out college photo IDs, as few colleges in Pennsylvania issue IDs that include an expiry date. This meant students had to go to the trouble of visiting the school bursar's office for a new ID before they could vote, which has the intended effect of reducing student turnout by the sponsors of this new law. Another quirk in the law was voters had to show a state-issued transportation ID on Election Day. The Republican Secretary of State assured the public that 99 percent of registered voters already had the correct state-issued photo ID, but this was a bold faced lie. The truth is that more than 750,000 registered voters lacked a driver's license. Most of the affected are minorities, and most of them likely to vote Democrat.

Even more absurd is the fact that in the states implementing these voter ID laws, one can buy a gun at a gun show or off the Internet with far less identification.

Here's where I think the biggest scandal lies: why isn't the mainstream media not reporting this blatant sabotage of the democratic process, especially when it's not like the Republican Party is hiding their strategy and its objective? I can't recall CNN ever once covering this orchestrated voter suppression. When Pennsylvania wrote this law into passage, the Republican House majority leader, Mike Turzai, bragged at a State Committee meeting, "Voter ID, which is going to allow Governor Romney to win the state of Pennsylvania: done!" This is a breathtaking pronouncement, and is a smoking gun if ever one was needed. In July 2013, Pennsylvania's GOP Chairman Rob Gleason appeared on Pennsylvania Cable Network (RCN) to boast that while Romney had lost the 2012 race, he did cut into the 10-point lead Obama won over John McCain. RCN host asked Gleason, "Do you believe the attention that was given to voter ID made a difference in the 2012 election?" Gleason replied, "We probably had a better election. Think about this, we cut Obama by 5 percent, which was big. A lot of people lost sight of that. He won, he beat McCain by 10 percent, he only beat Romney by 5 percent. I think that probably voter ID had helped a bit in that."

Pennsylvania is far from being a case in isolation, either. In Florida, voters in predominantly black precincts endured chaos and marathon-voting lines in 2012, thanks largely to reduced voting hours, voter registration restrictions, voter purges, and intimidation tactics. The *Palm Beach Post* reported several prominent Florida Republicans admitting election law changes were designed wholly with the purpose of suppressing minority and Democratic votes. Florida Governor Rick Scott claimed new voter laws in his state were designed to curb in-person voter fraud, despite the fact a person is more likely to be killed by a falling coconut in Florida than commit voter fraud. But Republican Party members confirmed the motive was to make it harder for Democrats and minorities to vote. Wayne Bertsch, who handles local and legislative races for Republicans, said he knew targeting Democrats was the goal. "In the races I was involved in 2008, when we started seeing the increase of turnout and the turnout operations that the Democrats were doing in early voting, it certainly sent a chill down our spines. And in 2008, it didn't have the impact that we were afraid of. It got close, but it wasn't the impact that they had this election cycle."

Another GOP consultant also confirmed that influential consultants to the Republican Party of Florida were intent on beating back Democratic turnout in early voting after 2008. "I know that the cutting out of the Sunday before Election Day was one of their targets only because that's a big day when the black churches organize themselves."

Jesus H. Fuck! Right there, in all of the above examples, are guilt free admissions that voter ID laws have nothing to do with protecting the integrity of the ballot box, but have everything to do with disenfranchising voters in order to win elections. In state after state this is happening. In state after state, Republicans are locking in religious tea-baggers so that their corporate sponsors can realize their ambitions: lower taxes and weaken regulation. It's truly terrifying to imagine the prospect whereby a majority of elected officials in this country are ruling with the agenda of overturning Roe v Wade, returning to a segregated education system while the NRA and the tobacco industry determine what is best for all of us.

This is how corporations and the religious theocrats aim to erode everything this country has ever accomplished. Nay, it's how they *are* accomplishing it. It's real and it's happening now. The media in their cowardice about presenting a false equivalency are failing to shine a spotlight on what is unarguably the greatest threat this democracy has ever faced. I'm not suggesting the Democratic Party are all angels; they are not. They are a party that has many ideological flaws, too. But there is simply *no* example of Democrats keeping voters from participating in this democracy. None!

Alexander Keyssar, a top voting rights scholar and author of *The Right to Vote*, writes:

> What is so striking about the wave of legislation for ID laws is that we are witnessing for the first time in more than a century, a concerted, multi-state effort to make it more difficult for people to exercise their democratic rights... It is very reminiscent of what occurred in the North between 1875 and 1910 – the era of Jim Crow in the South – when a host of procedural obstacles were put in the way of immigrants trying to vote.

What's more, it's happening all across the Union. Wisconsin and New Hampshire passed restrictive voter ID laws that make it almost impossible for someone without a driver's license to vote. All in all, in the two years between 2010 and 2012, Republican state legislatures introduced 140 bills to restrict voting. By the summer of 2012, 16 states had passed legislation, including key battleground states of Florida, Pennsylvania, Virginia, Colorado, and New Hampshire.

In North Carolina, Senate Republicans unveiled a new voter ID bill in July 2013 that would further restrict the forms of photo identification accepted at polling booths. The new measure eliminates more than half the types of photo identification allowed currently, including cards from University of North Carolina colleges, state community colleges, and private employers. The bill is expected to take full effect in the 2016 elections, and serves only to suppress the vote of college students and minorities, and other demographics that lean towards the Democrats. In the 2012 election, 76 percent of African American voters took advantage of early voting, as many of this demographic work shift work or minimum wage jobs that make voting on a specific Tuesday problematic. In fact, 1.2 million Democratic voters voted early in 2012, whereas only 800,000 Republicans did same. So guess what? The Republican Governor has said goodbye to early voting. The bill also eliminates same-day registration, and ends pre-registration for 16- and 17-year olds. Not only is this bill hostile to our nation's democratic values, it doesn't even have the support of a majority of people in North Carolina. Public Policy Polling found that only 39 percent of voters in the state support the voter ID laws, with more than 50 percent firmly opposed to them. But with the Republican Party having control of the Governor's mansion, and the legislature, who cares what the people think, right?

The Christian Right has a historical relationship with the Republican Party's war on voting. Paul Weyrich, the founding father of the Christian Right, told a gathering of evangelicals in 1980 that he wanted fewer people to vote because the more people who vote, the less leverage the Christian Right has. "I don't want everybody to vote. Elections are not won by a majority of people. They never have been from the beginning of our country, and they are not now. As a matter of fact our leverage in the elections quite candidly goes up as the voting populace goes down." Do atheists and progressives need any more evidence that we are being out-maneuvered?

Going forward, progressives, secularists, and atheists need to wake up to the importance of winning state legislative elections. If not, the uber conservative wing of the Republican Party will continue to win state legislatures, thus ensuring we remain an impotent minority in state politics. State law touches almost every aspect of how we live, and Republican legislatures have now used their minorities to shape those aspects in line with their ultra-conservative positions and false beliefs. For example, in red state legislatures everywhere, Republicans are launching an attack on women's reproductive rights. During the years 2011-13, two-dozen states adopted 178 anti-abortion restrictions. We know as matter of fact that access to healthcare improves women's economic conditions. But red legislatures are enacting laws that require women's clinics meet the same standards as hospital surgical standards, forcing many of these clinics to close down, mostly in rural areas. Republican controlled states have also passed severe anti-union measures, cut unemployment benefits, denied access to the Affordable Healthcare Act, among other attacks on safety net institutions.

CHAPTER FIVE

THE LORDS OF THE GAME

"We want to bear witness today that we know the relation between corporate greed and what goes on too often in the Supreme Court decisions."

CORNEL WEST

One can argue that the Supreme Court is the most powerful institution in America in terms of guiding the nation's ideological and cultural path. If you accept this premise, then it's impossible to overstate how devastating a blow the 2000 presidential election was to those who treasure the separation of Church and State, and equally to those who demand a separation of Corporations and State. Anyone who denies the Supreme Court has become a subsidiary of big corporations and the conservative agenda is suffering a severe case of cognitive dissonance.

The decision of the conservative majority Supreme Court to block a recount of Florida's votes on a 5-4 count, a truly ideological and politically biased move, handed George W. Bush the presidency, and left no doubt in any keen observer's mind that the nation's highest court is anything other than a political body. The Gore v Bush decision was especially monumental due to the then imminent likelihood that two of the justices on the Court would announce their retirement in the first decade of the new millennium. Essentially, a Gore presidency would have meant liberals held a majority in the court for the first time since pre-Nixon presidency. But as they say in the classics, winners are grinners, and losers can please themselves.

Justice Sandra Day O'Connor and Justice William Rehnquist retired in President Bush's second term. Bush replaced the outgoing justices with Samuel Alito and John Roberts, respectively. With Roberts' senate confirmation as Chief Justice, so began the reign of the most corporate and religious ideological court in modern times.

In declaring Citizens United the winner over the Federal Election Commission in 2010, the Court declared that corporations have the same rights as people, with unlimited rights to pour money into electing corporate candidates, who in turn protect their interests. Senator Charles Schumer (NY) declared of this ruling, "The bottom line is the Supreme Court has just predetermined the winners of next November's election. It won't be the Republicans or the Democrats and it won't be the American people: it will be Corporate America." (For the record, Schumer is a Wall Street sleaze, despite this useful quote)

Former U.S. President Jimmy Carter called it a "very stupid decision". Carter said that he and his Republican opponents used public financing to run their general election campaigns in 1976 and 1980.

"I would say that it's almost impossible for a candidate, like I was back in those days or others even, to be considered seriously as a candidate to represent the Democratic or Republican parties as nominee if you can't raise $100 million or $200 million from contributors, many of who know that they are making an investment in how they are going to be treated by the winner after the election is over. It's accepted fact," Carter said during a speech he gave in July of 2013. "It's legal bribery of candidates. And that repayment may be in the form of an ambassadorship to someone who has raised three or four hundred thousand dollars to help a candidate get elected."

A Supreme Court designed to protect our citizens has instead expanded the rights of powerful companies, working through the radical right majority led by Justices Roberts and Alito. The United States Supreme Court was founded to protect the American people, not big American corporations. Yet rulings in the Chief Justice Roberts era have allowed corporations to get away with paying women less than men, discriminating against the rights of older workers, dodging liability for faulty medical devices, ducking the Clean Water Act and avoid paying damages for the Exxon Valdez oil spill.

In a speech given to the American Constitution Society for Law, Senator Elizabeth Warren (D-MA) warns that interests representing America's biggest corporations are capturing the Supreme Court:

> Take a look at the win rate of the Chamber of Commerce. According to the Constitution Accountability Center, the Chamber moved from a 43 percent win rate during the very conservative Berger Court to a 56 percent win rate under the very conservative Rehnquist court. And now they are at a 70 percent win rate under the Roberts Court. Follow this pro-business trend to its obvious conclusion and you will end up with a Supreme Court that's a wholly-owned subsidary of the Chamber of Commerce.

This is a staggering trend with only one winner: super rich assholes!

Most of us think of the Chamber of Commerce as a breakfast get together of local business owners in a given community. That's how I thought of it, as I was once a member of a chamber many years ago. Today, however, the Chamber of Commerce is the nation's largest business lobby group. In 2012, it spent more than $100 million on lobbying Republican politicians. Aligned with the 501(c) "social welfare" non-profits that the Citizens United v FEC decision help breed virulently, the Chamber raised and spent more than one billion dollars to help shape the 2012 elections. Suddenly, the Chamber of Commerce seems a little less folksy.

For business, elections offer a far less reliable and predictable return on investment than does focusing on the courts. Doug Kendall of the Constitution Accountability Center says, "Overall, the Court will likely decide 76 cases this Term, meaning that the Chamber will have participated in roughly 24 percent of the Court's decided cases." Added to the Chamber's remarkable access is the fact that the Conservative justices side with the Chamber 82 percent of the time. Now, if you think this is a good thing for America, then you think unbridled deregulation is a sound economic strategy, because that's what this is all about. It's big business taking laws and regulations to task in the courts, so that they can maximize profits at all costs. A brief history lesson of deregulation looks a little something like this: in the years 1797 to 1944, the American banking system crashed once every 15 years. In 1933, congress put good reforms in place, of which the Glass-Steagall Act was the centerpiece. The result? Well, from 1933 to the early 1980s, a 50-year period, the number of banking crashes equaled *zero*! So, what happened after that? Well, you had the Reagan presidency start in 1980, and what followed was a 30-year period of continual de-regulation. We had the S&L crisis, followed by the crash of 1987, then the long-term capital management problem at the end of the 90s, which ultimately led all the way to the Great Recession that started in 2008. So yes, unrestrained corporatism is bad for this everyone in this country, out-side of those fortunate to be in the top 1 percent.

The Supreme Court's alignment with corporate inter-ests comes directly at the expense of the little guy. And by the little guy I mean all of us, and particularly minorities. Because if there's one thing corporate America needs to do in order to shepherd their Jesus freaks into office, it's to ensure left-leaning minorities cannot vote. And now we come to arguably the most blatant and subversive attack on black voters since Jim Crow laws in the 60s. You know, the whole "separate but equal" thing.

The Voting Rights Act of 1965 was implemented by congress under the President Johnson administration. It was a landmark piece of national legislation that effected laws against discrimination in voting. Essentially, the Act prohibits states from imposing any "voting qualification or prerequisite to voting, or standard, practice, or proce-dure... to deny or abridge the right of any citizen to vote on account of race or color." Specifically, the intention of the Act was to prohibit the practice of requiring otherwise qualified voters to pass literacy tests in order to register to vote, a tactic Southern states had implemented to limit the effect of African Americans at the polls. The law estab-lished extensive federal oversight of elections, meaning states with a history of discriminatory voting practices could not implement any change affecting voting without first obtaining approval from the Department of Justice, a process known as preclearance. The Act is widely recognized as a landmark in the civil rights movement, but that sentiment resulted in no sentimentality in the Roberts' Supreme Court of 2013.

On June 23, 2013, the Supreme Court effectively struck down the heart of the Voting Rights Act of 1965 by a 5-to-4 vote, thus freeing nine states, mostly in the South, to change election laws without advance federal approval. In other words, Republican controlled states now have *carte blanche* to enact whatever voter suppression laws they choose. The four liberal justices argued that racial discrimination had not yet been rooted out of voting, and that minorities continue to face barriers to voting in states with a history of racial discrimination. But all five conservatives on the bench thought otherwise. In other words, Chief Justice Roberts and co believe race is no longer an issue in American society today, based solely on the fact we elected a black president. Argue that to black folk who are arrested at a ratio of 4:1 whites when it comes to marijuana possession. Argue that to the minorities who are searched at a rate of nearly 10:1 over whites under New York's Stop & Frisk policing policy. Argue that race relations are just fine and dandy to the parents of Trayvon Martin. In a 2013 poll of Georgia Republicans, Paula Deen was found to be more popular than Martin Luther King. *That*'s how far we haven't come in race relations!

Justice Ruth Bader Ginsburg, a Clinton appointee to the Court, was so upset by the repeal of the Voting Rights Act that she said, "Dr. Martin Luther King Jr's legacy and the nation's commitment to justice had been disserved by today's decision." She said the focus of the Voting Rights

Act had properly changed from "first generation barriers to ballot access" to "second-generation barriers" like redistricting and laws requiring at large-voting in places with a sizable black minority. She said the Act had been highly successful in thwarting laws and policy designed to suppress minority votes.

Naturally, it took a snowflake in hell moment before Republicans went on the rampage to implement voter suppression laws that the Act had prevented them from legislating. Immediately following the Court's decision, Texas announced that a voter identification law, which had been blocked by a federal court on the ground that it would disproportionately affect black and minority voters, would go into immediate effect. Further, when it comes to the "art" of redistricting maps, Texas would no longer require federal approval.

In Alabama and Mississippi, Republican officials have begun enforcing voter identification laws. And many red states have moved to end early voting, which was especially popular among students and minority voters during the 2012 election. No wonder Republican politicians are outwardly applauding the Court's decision. Republican Governor of Louisiana Bobby Jindal boasted, "The Court recognized that states can fairly design our own district maps and run our own elections without the federal government." The irony obviously lost on him in that he himself is black.

As you can see, this is a Court that has no regard for anything but the interests of corporations and those who carry out their wishes, the Republican Party. So, how long before the Court begins to appease social conservatives with a repeal of Roe v Wade? How long before the minimum wage is deemed unconstitutional? How long before creationism can be taught in public classrooms? How long before citizens have to take a Christianity loyalty oath?

Cass R. Sunstein, author of *Radicals in Robes: Why Extreme Right-Wing Courts are Bad for America*, writes, "Our courts now represents the most extreme elements of the Republican Party. These reformers include a number of federal judges – radicals in robes, fundamentalists on the bench. Usually appointed by Ronald Reagan, George H.W. Bush, or George W. Bush, some of these judges do not hesitate to depart radically from longstanding understandings of constitutional meaning. Not only are they eager to understand the Second Amendment to protect the personal right to keep and bear arms; they are also willing to impose severe restrictions on Congress's power and to strike down affirmative action programs, campaign finance regulation, environmental regulations, and much else." Sunstein says the Republican Party move to reshape the Supreme Court has been an orchestrated effort. "Since the election of President Reagan, a disciplined, carefully orchestrated, and quite self-conscious effort by high-level Republican officials in the White House and the Senate has radically transformed the federal judiciary. For more than two decades, Republican leaders have had a clear agenda for the nation's courts, including the following major goals:

- To reduce the powers of the federal government, including Congress itself;
- To scale back the rights of those accused of crime;
- To strike down affirmative action programs;
- To eliminate campaign finance laws;
- To diminish privacy rights, above all the right to abortion;

- To invigorate the Constitution's Takings Clause in order to insulate property rights from democratic control;
- To forbid Congress from allowing citizens to bring suit to enforce environmental regulation;
- To protect commercial interests, including commercial advertisers, from governmental regulation.

The Republican Party has proactively sought out judicial candidates who they believe will interpret the Constitution and other federal statutes in a way that serves their radical agenda. An examination of the Roberts Court reveals ideological agenda-driven decisions on all of the hot-button issues that have come before it:

Race: (Parents v. Seattle & Meredith v. Jefferson). The Court ruled that local school districts cannot do anything to ensure racial diversity in their schools.

Abortion: (Gonzales v. Carhart). The Court upheld the federal partial-birth abortion ban.

Campaign Finance: (Citizens United vs. Federal Elections Commission). The Court ruled in favor of billionaires (Citizens United). Money equals free speech.

Equal Rights: (Ledbetter v. Goodyear). The Court's decision makes it harder for female employees to sue employers on equal-pay grounds.

Free Speech: (Morse v. Frederick). The Court ruled to limit free speech rights of students.

Punitive Damages: (Philip Morris v Williams). The Court overturned an Oregon court's decision that had awarded damages to an ex-smoker.

Immigration: (Lopez v Gonzales). The Court ruled that a non-citizen can be deported for committing a drug crime that's deemed by court to be a misdemeanor.

In all of the above rulings, with the exclusion of Lopez v. Gonzales, the justices delivered a 5 to 4 decision, with the same five judges in the majority on each occasion. As you can see, based on the above rulings, Sustein's words were quite prophetic.

In returning to the Voting Rights Act, thankfully there's an outlet to rewrite the provision that was struck down. The outlet is called the Congress. But with the GOP in control of the House, that's unlikely to happen, thus underscoring the importance of meeting the enthusiasm and agitation evangelicals and conservatives bring to the polls during mid-term and state elections.

Political analyst James Fallows wrote in *The Atlantic*:

> Normally I shy away from apocalyptic readings of the American predicament. We're a big, messy country; we've been through a lot – perhaps even more than we thought, what with Abraham Lincoln and the vampires. We'll probably muddle through this and be very worried about something else ten years from now. But when you look at the sequence from Bush v. Gore, through Citizens United, to what seems to be coming on the health-care front; and you combine it with ongoing efforts in Florida and elsewhere to prevent voting from presumably Democratic blocs; and add that to the simply unprecedented abuse of the filibuster in the years since the Democrats won control of the Senate and then took the White House, you have what

we'd identify as a kind of long-term coup if we saw it happening anywhere else.

Atheists and progressives can no longer afford to remain cynically apathetic. The American Taliban is taking control of the levers of power even though they are not aligned with America's cultural center. The stakes are getting higher. And the war is being fought on multiple fronts.

CHAPTER SIX

THE AMERICAN TALIBAN (GETTING VOTERS INTO THE GAME)

"Yes, religion and politics do mix. America is a nation based on biblical principles. Christian values dominate our government. The test of those values is the Bible. Politicians who do not use the Bible to guide their public and private lives do not belong in office."

BEVERLEY LAHAYE

In describing the Christian Right, I do like the moniker the American Taliban, for it so perfectly describes who and what they are. Who they are today is the Tea Party. In a recent Pew Research Poll, it was found that the Tea Party holds even stronger religious attitudes than the group who merely identifies themselves as social conservatives. The Christian Right and the Tea Party have much in common with their cousins in the mountains of tribal Afghanistan:

- Ideological purity. There is no room for moderation.
- Compromise is seen as weakness
- A fundamentalist belief in biblical literalism
- Denying science and undeterred by facts
- Hostile to progress
- A demonization of education
- A need to control women's bodies

- Homophobia
- Xenophobia
- Tribal mentality
- Intolerance of dissent
- Pathological hatred of the U.S. government

Moreover, it aptly describes how all-encompassing the radical white Christian movement is in this country. Think Fox News, Ann Coulter, Rush Limbaugh, Sarah Palin, Rick Santorum, George W. Bush and the entire neo-conservative movement. Think Ron Paul and his loony faux-libertarianism ideology; Michele Bachmann, Rick Perry, Ted Cruz, Pat Robertson, Mike Huckabee etc, etc. If they're not evangelizing their radical worldview with their constituencies, they are shoving it down their opponents' throats, usually unchallenged, on their ideological-friendly media outlets. In other words, they've created a parallel universe where dissent, facts, and rival opinion are denied airtime. A universe that is effectively one giant confirmation bias jumping castle. There is simply no equivalence in the liberal secular cosmos.

The unquestionable cornerstones of the American Taliban's worldview is that Christian America is the most culturally superior civilization on the planet, and anyone who challenges that assertion is a gay, liberal terrorist that hates America. It's strictly xenophobic mainstream culture that's central tenet amounts to totalitarianism for Jesus Christ. Which, of course, is no different to the totalitarianism beliefs of Islamic extremists throughout the Muslim world. Former Republican House Majority Whip Tom DeLay, whose political career ended for conspiring to rig an election in Texas, once addressed a large audience with, "Christianity offers the only viable, reasonable, definitive answer to the questions of 'Where did I come from?' 'Why am I here?' 'Where am I going?' 'Does life have any meaningful purpose?' Only Christianity offers a way to understand that physical and moral border. Only Christianity offers a comprehensive worldview that covers all areas of life and thought, every aspect of creation." Or when Ann Coulter said in the wake of 9/11, "We should invade their countries, kill their leaders, and convert them to Christianity."

Now, compare the rhetoric to that of the Ayatollah Ali Khameni, the theocratic leader of Iran:

> Our religion's message is in contradiction to the message spread by the devils of the world. Well, the devils find it hard to put up with that message. There are Satans in today's world too. They find it hard and, therefore, confront and challenge our message. There is no alternative to victory in this challenge and confrontation except by standing firm with faith. There is no alternative but to believe in ourselves and our chosen path. This is the only alternative. We must believe in our path. All the believers of this path must join hands and stand firm. We must demonstrate steadfastness. This is the path to progress and victory. If all the believers do so, their victory will be certain.

Of course, one could make an entire coffee table book of tit for tat Christian-Islamic quotes, as there are no shortages of profoundly disturbing proclamations on both sides, but the point is this, the American Taliban is not interested in supporting a flourishing democracy, much less our democracy. They hate our freedoms as much as the Afghanistan Taliban hates school children dancing in the streets to N-Sync. Their goal is often stated in sub-texts, but also unashamedly overtly. Take Gary Potter, president of Catholics for Christian Political Action, "After the Christian majority takes control, there will be no satanic churches, no more free distribution of pornography, no more talk of rights for homosexuals. After the Christian majority takes control, pluralism will be seen as immoral and evil and the state will not permit anybody the right to practice evil." Yes, holy fucking shit, indeed.

In his book *American Taliban*, Mark Moulitsas writes, "This level of intolerance is not the domain of loons and fringe dwellers but rather the very lifeblood coursing through the entire body of the modern conservative movement." Christian America is not in love with America, it's in love with this country subject to their leaders being in control of America. What makes the American Taliban the perfect vehicle for corporations to hijack this democracy is their rigid conformity and open hostility to free enquiry – extending far beyond the story of Noah's Ark in the Bible. Their craziness and willingness to accept mythical notions spill over into areas of domestic and foreign policy, which make them the perfect proxy ally for big business. Take the environment as one such example. The Christian Right has emerged as ready apologists for environmental polluters, and aggressive critics of policy designed to protect the environment. The Christian Right has given the GOP political cover to hammer away at state and federal environmental safeguards.

So how far is the Republican Party away from scientific reality when it comes to the matter of climate change? Well, consider that of the 48 newly elected GOP congressmen during the 2010 midterms, all but one was sworn into office as a climate change denier. (We can assume that "one" doesn't get many invitations from Big Oil sponsored "Coke & Hooker" junkets.) Moreover, the *National Journal* recently asked a group of Republican senators and House members: "Do you think it's been proven beyond a reasonable doubt that the earth is warming because of man-made problems?" Of the respondents, an overwhelming 77 percent said no. This result is consistent with a Pew Research Centre study, which showed that less than 25 percent of Christians believe global warming to be a real phenomenon.

Now compare the above conservative belief alongside that of people who actually may know a thing or two about climate change: the entire scientific community, whereby climate experts are virtually unanimous in the view that the planet is warming. In fact, of 2,000 scientists who contributed to a U.N. Intergovernmental Panel on Climate Change, more than 1,800 (90 percent) are certain in their belief of man-made global warming.

You see, scientists base their belief in facts and evidence, whereas Republican lawmakers base theirs in special interest PR literature ("Why Global Warming is Bunk" by Exxon) and campaign contributions; while Christians base theirs in the earth "science" found in the Bible. In fact, two Christian think tanks (I am aware of the oxymoron), Young-Earth Creationists and Answers in Genesis, recently released a brochure that read:

> The contention that man's activities are causing global warming, as described in the media and by its advocates, is a myth. There is no reason either biblically or scientifically to fear the exaggerated and misguided claims of catastrophe as a result of increasing levels of man-made carbon dioxide (CO_2).

The obvious question being, how could the Bible provide any insight on climate science, when climate science wasn't a thing at the time the Bible was written? As a matter of fact, the only "sciencey" things the Bible gets right is that birds fly, horses have four legs, water is wet, fish swim in the sea, the earth is flat and the sun goes to bed in its own tabernacle at night. Well, correct if you don't count the last two mistakes.

Buoyed by corporate finances and a radical "dominion theology", the Christian Right has become more aggressive and fanatical in its defense of corporations and denial of climate change. Moreover, the Christian Right is working to misrepresent the "green" movement as a dangerous liberal hoax that is harmful to the poor and a threat to Christianity.

The Cornwall Alliance for the Stewardship of Creation is a faith-based anti-environmental political action group. The group is led by E. Calvin Beisner, who believes that since God granted humans "dominion over the earth, humans have the right to exploit the plant by whatever means they see fit. So, who is the Cornwall Alliance? One thing it's not is a humble church group of delusional Christian fundamentalists. What it is, however, is a front group for the Committee for a Constructive Tomorrow (CFACT), which is an anti-environmental group that is funded by ExxonMobil, Chevron, and Gulf Oil. And guess who else? Yes, the Koch Brothers. Further, other sponsors of the Cornwall Alliance include the right wing political action committee groups, Americans for Tax Reform, Americans for Prosperity, and the Competitive Enterprise Institute.

In 2012, the Cornwall Alliance released a documentary called, *The Green Dragon*, which is a nickname the group uses to mock Christians who accept climate change as real. The group challenges that Christians who accept climate change are guilty of promoting a dangerous anti-Christian agenda. The documentary includes appearances by some of the most prominent personalities within the American Taliban movement: Bryan Fischer of the American Family Association, Tony Perkins of the Family Research Council, Tom Minnery of Focus For the Family, Wendy Wright of Concerned Women for America, Michael Farris of the Home School Legal Defense Association, and Janet Parshall – a Christian radio host. Some of the more quotable moments in the documentary include:

- **Janet Parshall:** "The Green Dragons have a lust for political power and spiritual deception. The environmental movement is deadly to the Gospel of Jesus Christ."
- **Bryan Fisher:** "Environmental movement is a threat to the Christian faith."
- **Tony Perkins:** "Environmentalists are pointing people away from God and into humanism and support of an unbiblical worldview."
- **E. Calvin Beisner:** "The green movement threatens liberty."
- **Michael Farris:** "Environmentalists are scaring little children to achieve their political ends."

In 2012, Beisner made a guest appearance on Glenn Beck's television show to claim that environmental protection is an attack against religion and humanity. Beck accused the green movement of holding "anti-human" beliefs and "worshiping the ancient god of Babylon, the god of weather", warning that "the progressive left is coming for the kill on religion". In 2013, Rush Limbaugh told his 30 million followers, "If you believe in God, you cannot intellectually believe in man-made global warming."

Increasingly, the GOP is echoing the 4,000-year-old "science" of groups like the Cornwall Alliance, as they wage war against the Environmental Protection Agency on behalf of their big corporate sponsors. In fact, both the Christian Right and the GOP are in lock step. Congressman John Shimkus (R-IL), who is now chairman of the Subcommittee on Environment and the Economy, during a 2009 hearing said:

> I want to start with Genesis 8, verse 21 and 22, *Never again will I curse the ground because of man, even though every inclination of his heart is evil from childhood, and never again will I destroy all living creatures as I have done. As long as the earth endures, sea time and harvest, cold and heat, summer and winter, day and night will never cease.* I believe that's the infallible word of God and that's the way it's going to be for His creation. The second verse comes from Matthew 24, *And He will send his Angels with a loud trumpet call and they will gather His elect from the Four Winds, from one end of the Heavens to the other.* The earth will end only when God declares it's time to be over. Man will not destroy the earth. This earth will not be destroyed by a flood.

Michele Bachmann (R-MN) said, "Nancy Pelosi is committed to her global warming fanaticism to the point where she has said that she's just trying to save the planet. We all know that someone did that over 2,000 years ago, they saved the planet – we didn't need Nancy Pelosi to do that."

Jim Inhofe (R-OK), who is the ranking member of the Environment and Public Works Committee said, "I really believe that a lot of people are in denial who want to hang their hat on the fact, that they believe is a fact, that man-made gases, anthropogenic gases, are causing global warming. The science really isn't there."

House Speaker John Boehner (R-OH) claimed that, "The idea that carbon dioxide is a carcinogen that is harmful to our environment is almost comical."

You'd think Republicans would've learnt a thing or two in the thirty years since President Reagan claimed, "Pollution comes from trees".

In 2011, congressional Republicans attempted to push through a bill that would repeal "the scientific determination by the EPA that CO_2 and other greenhouse-gas pollutants are a threat to human health and welfare", which prompted an objection from Democrat Senator Ed Markey, who openly mocked his Republican counterparts in the chamber:

> Mr. Chairman, I rise in opposition to a bill that overturns the scientific finding that pollution is harming our people and our planet.
>
> However, I won't physically rise, because I'm worried that Republicans will overturn the law of gravity, sending us floating about the room.
>
> I won't call for the sunlight of additional hearings, for fear that Republicans might excommunicate the finding that the Earth revolves around the sun.
>
> Instead, I'll embody Newton's third law of motion and be an equal and opposing force against

this attack on science and on laws that will reduce America's importation of foreign oil.

This bill will live in the House while simultaneously being dead in the Senate. It will be a legislative Schrodinger's cat killed by the quantum mechanics of the legislative process!

Arbitrary rejection of scientific fact will not cause us to rise from our seats today. But with this bill, pollution levels will rise. Oil imports will rise. Temperatures will rise.

And with that, I yield back the balance of my time. That is, unless a rejection of Einstein's Special Theory of Relativity is somewhere in the chair's amendment pile.

In their corner, the party of science deniers has a broad communications network. A study conducted by the Yale Project on Climate Communication suggests that regular exposure to right wing media explains why less than 25 percent of Republicans agree that human activity is causing global warming, despite the consensus of 97 percent of climate scientists. The study depicted five tactics right wing outlets use to erode trust in scientists:

1. Present contrarians as "objective" experts.
2. Denigrate peer-reviewed science and scientific institutions
3. Equate science with simply a liberal opinion
4. Claim scientists distort data in order to obtain funding
5. Characterize climate science as simply a "religion."

If the GOP had its way, and if it suited their corporate driven agenda, they'd vote to repeal gravity.

In *American Taliban*, Moulitsas writes that the relationship between the Christian Right and big business goes all the way back to the 1930s when an anti-unionist Methodist preacher, Abraham Vereide, claimed he had received a vision from God. Jeff Sharlet, author of *The Family*, writes, "God came to him [Vereide] one night in April 1935 and said Christianity had been focusing on the wrong people, the poor, the suffering and the out and out. God told him to be a missionary to and for the powerful." Vereide and his fellow evangelicals had become obsessed in their belief that democracy was the reason for America's ills. Instead, they looked to fascism for a solution, a religious fascism in what they called "Totalitarianism for Christ". Sharlet continues, "They predict that the United States will pretty quickly embrace this and will get rid of political parties because democracy doesn't work. They don't want a Republican Party, a Democratic Party. They want one party – theirs."

Moulitsas explains:

> This kind of evangelism had little to do with charity or nourishing the soul or connecting with God or becoming a better human being. That was for chumps. Rather, their Jesus was all about union busting and an aggressive, expansionist foreign policy. They began to organize prayer breakfast groups around the country, and over the next decade they succeeded in setting up groups in major cities and in the nation's seat of power on Capitol Hill. These evangelists operated under various monikers – the National Committee for Christian Leadership, the Fellowship House, and the International Foundation, among others – but were mostly identified as "The Family". The other benign

sounding, bureaucratic names helped mask The Family's secretive work: the cultivation as allies of the most influential and wealthy members of society, those in control of the levers of power... to this day, the organization boasts some of the top members of Congress and has sponsored the National Prayer Breakfast, which every president since 1953 has attended. At its heart, the Family is an elitist, anti-democratic effort, driven by its authoritarian and theocratic mission, but it isn't the only outpost of such thought in conservative circles. In fact, the nation's political right has been taken over by what can not so affectionately be called the American Taliban, a cabal of ideologues who are fundamentalist in their beliefs, intolerant of dissent and xenophobic in matters of foreign policy.

Today the Christian Right constitutes 30 percent of the voting population in America, with more than 50 percent residing in the South. We are talking about approximately 100 million Americans who are agitated, activated, and mobilized in a way that ensures their corporate puppet masters continue to harm the democratic ideals of this nation and its social well being. In looking again at the "two" Americas, nothing separates the North and South like religion. Dr. Michael Hill, president of the League of the South, the secessionist group he founded in 1994, says, "Of all things that divide the South from the rest of the country, the first one has got to be the fervent Christianity. The South historically has been a very Christian society. That has defined its worldview. We realize men have evil hearts and can't be trusted." If that isn't a sufficiently succinct summation of southern religiosity, then consider the writings of a greater authority. The University of Mississippi published the *Encyclopedia of Southern Culture*. The cover is deep-fried and delicious. It states, "The South is the only society in Christendom where the evangelical family of Christians is dominant... making the South the 'religious region' that it is and marking off the South from patterns, practices and perspectives prevalent in other parts of America." Problem is, they want to make the other parts of America look like theirs.

The South is to radical Christianity what radical Islam is to Afghanistan. A 2011 Barna Group study titled *Diversity of Faith in Various U.S. Cities* found that cities with the highest proportion of residents who describe themselves as Christian are all in the South. These include Shreveport (98 percent), Birmingham (96 percent), Charlotte (96 percent) and Greenville (94 percent).

Conversely, the cities of twenty-first enlightenment include the cities of the Yankee North and their Pacific Coast secular brethren: New York, Boston, Los Angeles, San Francisco, Seattle, and Portland.

It's not just that an overwhelming majority of Christians live in the South, it's the religious intensity they bring to their political attitudes. In 2009, a Pew Forum *Importance of Religion* study measured the degree of religious fervor in all 50 states of the country. It found that nine of the 10 most religious states are in the South. The tenth is another of the Republican strongholds: Oklahoma.

Their level of passion is inversely proportionate to our passivity. We are talking about tens of millions of Americans who seek to establish a utopian society based on Bronze Age ideals. They desperately desire to transform our secular society into a Christian theocracy. With the backing of hundreds of millions of corporate dollars, they have gained stupendous power in the last few years. Simply, they're as active and as aggressive as they have ever been before. The past year has seen a record number of anti-abortion bills put forward by these elected radicals, and that's just the start. Expect bigoted crusades against immigrants, Muslims, gays, atheists, and liberals in the immediate future. They are in control of our courts, and our legislative assemblies. Their only real opposition is us, but we have proven to be feckless, timid, and meek. A hostile counter-insurgency is needed to save our democracy.

CHAPTER SEVEN

WAR ON THE POOR (PART 1)

"If you're not careful, the newspapers will have you hating the people who are being oppressed, and loving the people who are doing the oppressing."

MALCOLM X

In the early 1960s, the national poverty rate was around 19 percent. On January 8, 1964, President Lyndon B. Johnson delivered his State of the Union speech:

> Let this session of Congress be known as the session which did more for civil rights than the last hundred sessions combined; as the session which enacted the most far-reaching tax cut of our time; as the session which declared all-out war on human poverty and unemployment in these United States; as the session which finally recognized the health needs of all our older citizens; as the session which reformed our tangled transportation and transit policies; as the session which achieved the most effective, efficient foreign aid program ever; and as the session which helped to build more homes, more schools, more libraries, and more hospitals than any single session of Congress in the history of our Republic.
>
> All this and more can and must be done. It can be done by this summer, and it can be done without any increase in spending. In fact, under the budget that I shall shortly submit, it can be done with an

actual reduction in Federal expenditures and Federal employment.

We have in 1964 a unique opportunity and obligation – to prove the success of our system; to disprove those cynics and critics at home and abroad who question our purpose and our competence.

If we fail, if we fritter and fumble away our opportunity in needless, senseless quarrels between Democrats and Republicans, or between the House and the Senate, or between the South and North, or between the Congress and the administration, then history will rightfully judge us harshly. But if we succeed, if we can achieve these goals by forging in this country a greater sense of union, then, and only then, can we take full satisfaction in the State of the Union.

Thus launching the phrase The War on Poverty, Johnson's address launched a number of initiatives including the creation of Medicare and Medicaid, the Food Stamp program, and the Economic Opportunity Act. By the way, you only get to call the Affordable Health Act - "ObamaCare" if you also call Medicare "JohnsonCare", and Social Security "FDRCare".

Predictably, the conservative backlash against expansion of the federal government came. Criticism also came from the left, for it was the time of the Vietnam War and many on the left could see that it was hypocritical to talk about fighting poverty at home while simultaneously funneling billions of dollars from the budget to wage a needless war abroad. Dr. Martin Luther King, in a speech on April 4, 1967, tied the war in Vietnam to the war on poverty:

> There is at the outset a very obvious and almost facile connection between the war in Vietnam and

the struggle I, and others, have been waging in America. A few years ago there was a shining moment in that struggle. It seemed as if there was a real promise of hope for the poor – both black and white – through the poverty program. There were experiments, hopes, new beginnings. Then came the buildup in Vietnam and I watched the program broken and eviscerated as if it were some idle political plaything of a society gone mad on war, and I knew that America would never invest the necessary funds or energies in rehabilitation of its poor so long as adventures like Vietnam continued to draw men and skills and money like some demonic destructive suction tube. So I was increasingly compelled to see the war as an enemy of the poor and to attack it as such. Perhaps the more tragic recognition of reality took place when it became clear to me that the war was doing far more than devastating the hopes of the poor at home.

While President Johnson's aims in fighting poverty were just, Dr. King's broader discussion of the conditions that cause poverty were far more salient. All in all, progressives worked together to fight what remains the largest and most visible scar on the face of America today. But programs and dialogues that speak to fighting poverty are not policies and legislation that warm the hearts of corporations and conservatives, for it not only implies the funding of social safety nets, it also means better work conditions for employees, such as collective bargaining, health care, and a higher and more just minimum wage. You know, all the things that wanton corporate greed and excess despise. So, a Reagan presidency that began in 1980 gave corporations the opportunity they had so long craved – the opportunity to roll back every initiative of FDR's New Deal and LBJ's Great Society. In 1976, the then candidate Reagan telegraphed what would define the Republican position on the War on Poverty for the next four decades and counting when he told the story of a woman from Chicago's South Side who was arrested for welfare fraud:

> She has 80 names, 30 addresses, 12 Social Security cards and is collecting veterans' benefits on four non-existing deceased husbands. And she is collecting Social Security on her cards. She's got Medicaid, getting food stamps, and she is collecting welfare under each of her names. Her tax-free cash income is over $150,000.

In response to Reagan's speech, Susan Douglas, a professor at the University of Michigan, wrote, "He specialized in the exaggerated, outrageous tale that was almost always unsubstantiated, usually false, yet so sensational that it merited repeated recounting... And because his 'examples' of welfare queens drew on existing stereotypes of welfare cheats and resonated with news stories about welfare fraud, they did indeed gain real traction."

Notwithstanding the fact that Reagan's words were yet another example of another of his favorite pastimes: dog whistle racism, Reagan didn't mention the welfare queen's race, but he didn't need to. White Southern voters had already painted a picture in their own minds. In their minds, they associate welfare with minorities. The birth of the catchphrase "welfare queen" was made, and it became a part of the Right's lexicon from that speech to now. It would frame the Right's attitude towards the War on Poverty in defining the enemy not as poverty itself, but the poor themselves. The Reagan Conservatives sought to establish a top-down coalition with big business and the white Christian Right. So began the trickle down fairy nonsense, which would come to wreak havoc on America's middle class for the next three decades and more.

But, like the myth of voter ID fraud, claims of widespread welfare fraud are equally fallacious. Erin O'Brien, a poverty expert at the University of Massachusetts, says, "The myth of the Cadillac-driving welfare queen who defrauds the system lingers even though there's no proof of it." Peter Berson, assistant chief of the government fraud unit in the Philadelphia District Attorney's Office says, "Welfare fraud among Philadelphia's 95,456 recipients is minute. The rate of welfare fraud is so low as to almost not be worth mentioning." But the reason it is mentioned is because it speaks to the narrative of big corporations – that the rich are hard-working job creators, and the poor are dishonest moochers. It was a theme carried by the 2012 Romney-Ryan campaign, the theme's implication being that America is afflicted with millions of lazy moochers who want to sponge off the hard work of the righteous; that the poor aren't underpaid and unemployed, they're just lazy and don't take personal responsibility. One Romney ad featured the words, "Under Obama's plan, you wouldn't have to work and wouldn't have to train for a job. They just send you a welfare check. And welfare-to-work goes back to being plain old welfare." Terry O'Niell, President, National Organization for Women, wrote a column in response to this ad that read, "That's right – low-income moms, disproportionately women of color, are the villains in this decades-old, deceitful and divisive ploy to win party allegiance and votes. It's this kind of thinking that allows Romney and Ryan to initiate such a reckless attack on Medicaid. If the people you're hurting with your policies are blameworthy - irresponsible loafers and swindlers who think they're entitled to health care, food, housing, you name it - then it's ok to punish them, right?"

And then came the gift that kept on giving for the Obama campaign, the "47 percent" remark that was caught by Pourley's hidden camera in what was intended to be an off camera speech to wealthy donors. Romney said:

> There are 47 percent of the people who will vote for the president no matter what. All right, there are 47 percent who are with him, who are dependent upon government, who believe that they are victims, who believe that government has a responsibility to care for them, who believe that they are entitled to health care, to food, to housing, to you name it. That that's an entitlement. And the government should give it to them. And they will vote for this president no matter what. And I mean, the president starts off with 48, 49, 48 — he starts off with a huge number. These are people who pay no income tax. Forty-seven percent of Americans pay no income tax. So our message of low taxes doesn't connect. And he'll be out there talking about tax cuts for the rich. I mean that's what they sell every four years. And so my job is not to worry about those people — I'll never convince them that they should take personal responsibility and care for their lives.

Notwithstanding the obvious callousness and vindictiveness of Romney's remarks, it's factually and fundamentally flawed. He claims the poor pay no income tax, but the truth of the matter is the poor pay more tax, in terms of percentage of their income, than the rich. The working poor have payroll taxes. Some pay approximately 7 percent of their wages to Social Security. In every state with the exception of Vermont, the poor pay a higher percentage on state and local taxes. There are also pay sales taxes, property taxes, and gas taxes. But the Romney-Ryan plan was to make the poor pay more taxes while giving further tax breaks to the super rich. MSNBC commentator Ed Schultz called the Romney-Ryan plan a "virtual battlefield map in the Republican war on the poor. It takes $5.3 trillion from programs benefiting low-income people. It gives a $4.3 trillion tax cut to the wealthiest in the country." The Republican budget plan to make room for cuts for the super rich includes gutting $770 billion from Medicaid, $205 billion from Medicare, $1.6 trillion from ObamaCare, and $2 trillion from a combination of programs that includes food stamps, federal pensions, and welfare. Even post 2012-election, the Republican plan is take two-thirds of its non-military spending cuts from low-income programs like food stamps, Medicaid, job training, and Pell grants for college. All this to make room for a tax cut of 25 percent for the rich. The non-partisan Tax Policy Center reported that taxes for those who make $30,000 or less would go up. Robert Greenstein, the president of the Centre on Budget Policy and Priorities, calls it, "Likely, the largest redistribution of income from the bottom to the top in modern U.S. history."

Worse, their budget policy is merely the spearhead of the war on the poor. Another battle that big corporations are asking their political proxies to fight is the one against the minimum wage. So, now, despite the fact that corporations are sitting on record profits and record cash reserves and are paying what are historically low tax rates, the GOP claims business needs to repeal the minimum wage, claiming business cannot afford it in a soft economy. In other words, despite sitting on a record $2 trillion cash and record annual profits, corporations cannot afford to pay their workers more than $7.25 per hour, which, for a 40-hour week, is below the poverty level. Look, if your business model depends on paying your workers a salary that they cannot survive on, then your business model should be outlawed. It's an age-old, simplistic Conservative argument that any increase in wages means lost jobs. But America grew rapidly in the 1950s and 1960s when the minimum age was comparatively much higher than it is today.

Today, the minimum wage is $7.25 per hour. But according to a 2013 study by the Center for Economic and Policy Research, the minimum wage should now be $21.72 if it kept up with increases in worker productivity. Even on a pure inflationary comparison, sans productivity, wageworkers should be earning a minimum of $10.25 per hour. But $10 per hour is still too high a price to pay for the corporations, apparently. If corporations had their way the minimum wage would be a pat on the back and a bag of mixed candy. In fact, Republicans rejected President Obama's proposal of a $9 per hour wage. In part because it was Obama who proposed it! You know, a black dude. Anyway, as a result, wages and salaries now make up the lowest share of the nation's gross domestic product since the government began recording the data in 1947. That's a 50 plus-year low! At the opposite end of the income spectrum, however, the investment bank UBS, described the current period as the "golden era of profitability".

Also consider that in 1950 a home cost four times a minimum wage yearly salary and the minimum wage was at $7.27 when adjusted for inflation. In 2013, a home costs 17.5 times a minimum wage yearly salary and the minimum wage is 2 cents less than in 1950. But that's not low enough for fat cats like the Koch brothers, who claim that doing away with the minimum wage requirement would actually benefit the poor:

> We want to do a better job of raising up the disadvantaged and the poorest in this country, rather than saying, "Oh, we're just fine now." We're not saying that at all. What we're saying is, we need to analyze all these additional policies, these subsidies, this cronyism, this avalanche of regulations, all these things that are creating a culture of dependency. And like permitting, to start a business, in many cities, to drive a taxicab, to become a hairdresser. Anything that people with limited capital can do to raise themselves up, they keep throwing obstacles in their way. And so we've got to clear those out. **Or the minimum wage.** Or anything that reduces the mobility of labor.

This prompted Stephen Colbert to joke, "He's right. Having to pay your employees really hurts small business. I mean, look at our nation's forefathers. Many arrived with nothing but the blouse on their back, but thanks to no minimum wage they started a booming cotton industry."

The bottom line is you, me and everyone else earning less than $250,000 per year is being royally and properly fucked by big business and the people who do their bidding: the GOP and the Christian Right. Robert Reich, former Labor Secretary under Clinton, says that, "Putting more money in the pockets of the country's lowest earners is not only fair, it would also help boost the economy. Fifteen million workers would get a pay rise, allowing them to buy more and thereby keeping others working." So not only is GOP policy dire for the poor, it's also bad for America.

Today, 46 million Americans live in poverty, or 15 percent of the population. Some 20 percent of all children live in poverty. Nearly 40 percent of black children do. But in 2013, the Republican controlled congress passed a bill to cut the Supplemental Nutrition Assistance Program (SNAP), formerly food stamps, by nearly $40 billion over the next 10 years. Boy, I had no idea the poor were fraudulently trading their food stamps for those Wall Street derivatives that crashed the entire fucking economy. This is a new shameful low for the Grand Old Party. A remarkable achievement given their recent concentrated efforts to suppress minority voters; eliminate women's reproductive rights; destroy public education; neuter labor protection laws; repeal affordable healthcare for 30 million Americans. I doubt there's a morally low enough bar they cannot limbo under.

More sickening is the fact the House vote came the day after the DOW reached a record high. In other words, the Republican Party celebrated further Wall Street excess by cutting a program that feeds low-income families with children where the parent(s) work for a living but don't make enough to adequately feed their families. If America needed a reminder that 95 percent of all income gains since 2009 have gone to the top 1 percent, they got one. In other words, life's good for those who drove the economy into a ditch with wanton, unsupervised greed that came at the end of three decades of Reagan's holy trinity: deregulation, privatization, and free trade.

The greatest irony in all of this is the Right's love of Jesus Christ! I don't recall Jesus being a union buster, and I don't remember him calling the poor lazy. In fact, Jesus said to "give to the poor, so you will have treasure in heaven." Further, his earliest supporters were the rural poor of Galilee and Judea. For conservatives, there's also that awkward passage whereby Jesus says that it's almost, if not completely impossible for a rich person to get into Heaven. The New Testament contains more than 300 verses dedicated to the poor and social injustice. In all, Jesus is clearly concerned for both, so the question becomes why aren't those who ask WWJD in their daily lives? Because it's doubtful whether Jesus, if he returned today, would defund those programs designed to help the poor the most: healthcare, food stamps, welfare, etc. It's funny that the Christian Right forgets that Jesus was a liberal Jew who gave away free booze and healthcare.

Republican Jesus, however, is an asshole! And their asshole-ness permeates though their chief source of information, Fox News, whereby their proudly Christian talk show hosts constantly malign the poor. In 2012, the conservative think tank, the Heritage Foundation, released a report on how the ownership of household appliances demonstrates that "most of the persons whom the government defines as 'in poverty' are not poor in any ordinary sense of the term." Bill O'Reilly took this obscenely inaccurate and agenda-slanted report to mock the poor, "How can you be so poor and have all this stuff?" Co-network host Stuart Varney weighed in on the report: "The image we have of poor people as starving and living in squalor really is not accurate. Many of them have things, what they lack is the richness of spirit. That's my opinion."

You see, blaming America's economic problems on the poor rather than on policies that favor the super rich and corporations is a strategy that ties in perfectly with religious ideology, because it's a mainstream Christian position to associate poverty with sin – the idea that those living in poverty are being punished for their sinful ways. They also blame tornados on gay sex.

The twisted irony is that if there truly is a welfare queen, it's a corporate welfare queen. As Stephen Colbert joked, "If poor people want food stamps, they should become a corporation," because corporations continue to receive subsidies, handouts, bailouts, and tax breaks that cost this country better roads, schools, airports, services and hospitals. Ultimately, we all pay the price for corporate cronyism in Washington. I don't pretend to be an economist, so here's the *New Yorker*'s pithy snapshot of corporate welfare in America today:

> From the days of high tariffs and giant land grants to the railroads, business and government have always been tightly intertwined in this country. But, in recent decades, what you could call the corporate welfare state has become bigger. Energy companies lease almost forty million acres of onshore land in the U.S. and more than forty million offshore, and keep the lion's share of the profits from the oil and natural gas that they pump out. In theory, this is O.K., because we get paid for the leases and we get royalties on what they sell, but in practice it often works differently. In 1996, for instance, the government temporarily lowered royalties on oil pumped in the Gulf of Mexico as a way of encouraging more drilling at a time of low oil prices.

But this royalty relief wasn't rescinded when oil prices started to rise, which gave the oil companies a windfall of billions of dollars. Something similar happened in the telecom industry in the late nineties, when the government, in order to encourage the transition to high-def TV, simply gave local broadcasters swathes of the digital spectrum worth tens of billions of dollars. In the mining industry, meanwhile, thanks to a law that was passed in 1872 and never rewritten, companies can lease federal land for a mere five dollars an acre, and then keep all the gold, silver, or uranium they find; we, the people, get no royalty payments at all. Metal prices have soared in the last decade, but the only beneficiaries have been the mine owners.

In other cases, the government offers direct subsidies, like those that have helped keep many renewable-energy projects afloat. Farmers, despite food prices at record highs, still receive almost five billion dollars annually in direct payments, along with billions more in crop insurance and drought aid. U.S. sugar companies benefit from the sweetest boondoggle in business: an import quota keeps American sugar prices roughly twice as high as they otherwise would be, handing the industry guaranteed profits.

The tax code, too, is a useful tool for helping businesses. Domestic manufacturers collectively get a tax break of around twenty billion dollars a year. State and local governments give away seventy billion dollars annually in tax breaks and subsidies in order to lure (or keep) companies. The strategies make sense for local communities keen to generate new jobs, but, from a national perspective, since they usually just reward companies moving from one state to another, they're simply giveaways.

These corporate welfare queens are the true fraudulent recipients of welfare in this country. You see, poor people don't have lobbyists. Corporations have lobbyists and they buy (bribe) their masters political favors such as fewer regulations, lower taxes, and the creation of tax loopholes. This is income taken from our national budget, which creates a hole that needs to be filled from elsewhere. Unfortunately, the elsewhere is the things that make our society better, like services for the poor, investment in infrastructure to grow our economy, and money towards our future i.e. education.

In 2011, Citizens for Tax Justice released a report that looked at 280 corporations, all of them Fortune 500 companies. What it found is that while the corporate income tax rate is 35 percent, the 280 corporations in the study paid less than half that amount, on average. Moreover, those who paid even half the corporate tax rate paid far more than many of their competitors. In fact, in the three-year period 2008 to 2010, 78 corporations had at least one year where they paid *zero* federal income tax, while 30 corporations paid not a single cent over the entire three years. What's even more damning is the fact that those 30 corporations that paid nothing, realized more than $160 billion in profits over that period. But instead of paying $55 billion in income taxes, which is what the 35 percent tax rate requires, these companies generated so many excess tax breaks that they reported negative taxes, and even received a tax rebate check totaling $21.8 billion. How does that benefit America?

Anyway, here is your list of scoundrels:

30 Corporations Paying No Total Income Tax in 2008-2010

Company ($-millions)	08-10 Profit	08-10 Tax	08-10 Rate
Pepco Holdings	882	-508	-57.6%
General Electric	10,460	-4,737	-45.3%
Paccar	365	-112	-30.5%
PG&E Corp.	4,855	-1,027	-21.2%
Computer Sciences	1,666	-305	-18.3%
NiSource	1,385	-227	-16.4%
CenterPoint Energy	1,931	-284	-14.7%
Tenet Healthcare	415	-48	-11.6%
Atmos Energy	897	-104	-11.6%
Integrys Energy Group	818	-92	-11.3%
American Electric Power	5,899	-545	-9.2%
Con-way	286	-26	-9.1%
Ryder System	627	-46	-7.3%
Baxter International	926	-66	-7.1%
Wisconsin Energy	1,725	-85	-4.9%
Duke Energy	5,475	-216	-3.9%
DuPont	2,124	-72	-3.4%
Consolidated Edison	4,263	-127	-3.0%
Verizon Communications	32,518	-951	-2.9%
Interpublic Group	571	-15	-2.6%
CMS Energy	1,292	-29	-2.2%
NextEra Energy	6,403	-139	-2.2%
Navistar International	896	-18	-2.0%
Boeing	9,735	-178	-1.8%
Wells Fargo	49,370	-681	-1.4%
El Paso	4,105	-41	-1.0%
Mattel	1,020	-9	-0.9%
Honeywell International	4,903	-34	-0.7%
DTE Energy	2,551	-17	-0.7%
Corning	1,977	-4	-0.2%
TOTAL	**$ 160,341**	**$ -10,742**	**-6.7%**

Naturally, corporate welfare is not necessarily a bad thing. Some of these subsidies and government loans result in favorable results for the economy at large, as seen by the success of electric car company Tesla Motors, which is a company Fox News crowed would fail, but not only has Tesla turned a profit, it also paid off the entire loan awarded to the company by the Department of Energy in 2010, with interest. As you can see, companies that benefit from corporate welfare are just as dependent as the families that cannot survive on the minimum wage or without welfare services like Planned Parenthood. Republicans say they want small government, but what they want is a government that's small when it comes to helping people and big when it comes to helping business. Let that hypocritical irony wash over you. A playing field that only favors the rich and influential, and one that only widens the wealth gap between the middle class and the rich is a real and present threat to not only our democracy but also to our collective well-being. Reich, in the documentary *Inequality for All*, warns that, "Losers in rigged games can become very angry. We're seeing an entire society that is starting to pull apart."

It's astonishing that the disastrous collapse of the free market economy in 2008 has heralded a popular revival of the far right. In times of old, a collapse of irresponsible and corrupt capitalism ushered in a revival of the left. In his book *Pity the Billionaire*, Thomas Frank writes:

> When catastrophe comes, the thirties taught us, certain legislative deeds will follow swiftly. Unemployment insurance will be extended, and extended again. There will be massive investment in public works. Commissions will be named to investigate

the causes of the crisis. Agencies will be set up to keep people from losing their houses to foreclosures. Those hurt by the downturn will start to take action themselves. Union organizing and a wave of strikes will sweep the country in response to the complete breakdown of capitalism.

Outside of the short-lived Occupy movement, however, the loudest response to the complete failure of unrestrained capitalism has come from those who blame the poor, government, and workers. Surely making this the most pitiful irony in the years that followed the end of President George W. Bush's presidency. For the nation's second most catastrophic collapse was exclusively caused by Wall Street and the Reagan-esq economic policies that removed all government oversight of the financial market. Frank refers to this doctrine as the gospel of deregulation.

> Under the guidance of this doctrine, Federal authorities removed certain derivatives from regulatory oversight; they watered down requirements that banks balance their risk with safe assets; they exempted credit default swaps from regulation as insurance products; they dialed back the Federal Reserve's regulatory powers; they struck down a rule that required hedge-fund advisers to register with the Securities and Exchange Commission, and they pre-empted efforts by state governments to crack down on predatory lending.

But somehow the Tea Party and the Christian Right have bought into the corporate myth that the crash was caused by the poor, the lazy, and the people who protect them – government and unions. At any Tea Party rally you hear the rallying cry, "What do we say to Socialism?" The crowd yells, "Boooo!" "What do we say to capitalism?" The crowd yells, "Yayyyy!" The preamble of the 2009 Tea Party manifesto, the "Contract from America", states, "The most powerful, proven instrument of material and social progress is the free market."

In a 2009 Tea Party pamphlet called *Spread This Wealth*, the author, C. Jesse Duke explains the nature of capitalism by illustrating the doings of an imaginary primitive man who finds a stick, kills a deer, and trades things with other primitive men. Duke then makes the following pronouncement:

> This whole process of free markets and the trading of time and energy is just the natural order of the world. A tree exchanges oxygen for carbon dioxide. A fire exchanges heat for oxygen. Atoms exchange electrons to become atoms. Plants collect light to make chlorophyll, which nourishes animals, which become food for other animals and man, and so on. Everything in nature is constantly exchanging. So the free exchange of time and energy between people is the God-designed natural order. Conflicts erupt when the order is upset.

Duke's narrative appeals to those who like simple-sounding solutions for complex problems, for it implies that God Himself wants government to stay out of the way of capitalism. Of course, not only is Duke's narrative no more sophisticated than *The Pet Goat*, the experience of capitalism has never reflected that fairy tale. A government free market is something not even businesses want. A famous historian, Sidney Lens, wrote, "Not a single major American industry could survive today without government." Corporations are dependent on their subsidies, competitive protection laws, grants, and bailouts.

That the "free market" is natural and inevitable, existing outside and beyond government control is one of the most deceptive ideas continually echoed by the Right. According to this corporate-driven nonsense, governments shouldn't intrude through minimum wages, investments in public spending, taxes on high earners, regulations, or anything else, because the "free market" knows best. Robert Reich writes:

> In reality, the "free market" is a bunch of rules about (1) what can be owned and traded (the genome? slaves? nuclear materials? babies? votes?); (2) on what terms (equal access to the internet? the right to organize unions? corporate monopolies? the length of patent protections?); (3) under what conditions (poisonous drugs? unsafe foods? deceptive Ponzi schemes? uninsured derivatives? dangerous workplaces?) (4) what's private and what's public (police? roads? clean air and clean water? healthcare? good schools? parks and playgrounds?); (5) how to pay for what (taxes, user fees, individual pricing?). And so on. In short, these rules don't exist in nature; they are human creations. Moreover, governments don't "intrude" on free markets; governments organize and maintain them. Markets aren't "free" of rules; the rules define them.

But, of course, the Christian Right remains wholly ignorant to these kinds of facts and reality. In their eyes, to be rich and powerful is to demonstrate God's providence. To be poor is to demonstrate sinfulness, and while the Christian Right continues to dominate the GOP's agenda, and in turn the GOP controls the nation's agenda, a sensible discussion on tackling the nation's economic struggles will continue to be fruitless because conservatives love nothing more than the mythical romanticism of "rugged individualism".

WAR ON THE POOR (PART 2)

"I am convinced that imprisonment is a way of pretending to solve the problem of crime. It does nothing for the victims of crime, but perpetuates the idea of retribution, thus maintaining the endless cycle of violence in our culture. It is a cruel and useless substitute for the elimination of those conditions - poverty, unemployment, homelessness, desperation, racism, greed -which are at the root of most punished crime. The crimes of the rich and powerful go mostly unpunished."

HOWARD ZINN

One of the most terrifying facts I discovered in researching this book was that corporations like American Express and General Electric, and investment banks like Smith Barney, are now owners of prisons in this country. While I had always known the expansion of the industrial prison complex to be broad, I had no clue that it was *that* broad, which makes this the most audacious and inhumane quasi-military offensive waged against the poor since the commencement of the slave trade in America in the 1600s.

In 2013, there are 2.5 million Americans behind bars, which means roughly 1 in every 100 Americans are incarcerated in any given year with another 5 million on probation or parole. Further striking is the fact that while people of color make up 30 percent of the population, they represent more than 60 percent of the behind bars population. Our incarceration rates are higher than any other country on the planet. So, what is going on?

Well, what's going on is that the Christian Right's uncompromising, overly simplified, and unsophisticated view of crime has allowed Republican politicians to pave the way for big corporations to profit from putting our citizens behind bars. The prison industrial complex is an interweaving of business and government interests. It serves to feed two private purposes: profit and social control. Its publicly stated purpose, however, is to fight crime and to keep violent criminals off our streets, but that's a self-serving lie. Despite the efforts of Fox News to keep you in fear of Muslims, terrorists, drug users, and serial killers, violence occurs in less than 14 percent of reported crime, and injuries occur in less than 3 percent. The top three charges for those entering prison are: drug possession, sale of drugs, and robbery. Violent crimes don't even feature in the top 10 reasons for incarceration. But in the same way that fear of immigrants and Islam is a boom for the military industrial complex, the fear of "random violence" is great for the for-profit prison business.

Two-time Pulitzer winner Steven Pinker says that despite the ceaseless news about war, crime, and terrorism, western civilization is living in the most peaceable era in the existence of our species. In his book, *The Better Angels of our Nature,*' Pinker draws on a ton of analytical data to support his hypothesis:

> The decline, to be sure, has not been smooth. It has not brought violence down to zero, and it is not guaranteed to continue. But it is a persistent historical development, visible on scales from millen-

nia to years, from the waging of wars to the spanking of children. No aspect of life is untouched by the retreat from violence. Daily existence is very different if you always have to worry about being abducted, raped, or killed, and it's hard to develop sophisticated arts, learning, or commerce if the institutions that support them are looted and burned as quickly as they are built.

Unfortunately, today's media works on the commercial theory, 'If it bleeds, it leads'. As such, our never-ending exposure to what are rare incidences of violence serves to keep us afraid and distort our reality. It also serves to garner support for unnecessarily draconian crime policies, which serve to benefit the corporate owners of the prison industry.

The nation's largest private prison company is Corrections Corporation of America (CCA). If you wish to participate in the modern day slave trade you can buy shares in CCA on the New York Stock Exchange under the ticker code: CXW. With a war chest of more than $300 million, the corporation intends to grow its core business, locking up black dudes, by buying every state penitentiary in the U.S. Glen Ford, President of Black Agenda Radio said, "The Corrections Corporation of America believes the economic crisis has created an historic opportunity to become the landlord, as well as the manager, of a big chunk of the American prison gulag." In July of 2013, CCA announced to the NYSE that it would be paying a massive dividend of $675 million to its shareholders.

Imagine what happens when one corporation, or just a few corporations, own all the state prisons. It means they can set the prices without open-bid competition. Much in the same way that companies like Haliburton have the privilege of doing, which ultimately means "we the people" pay more for their products and services. Worse, the interests of private prisons are not aligned with the interests of a healthy functioning society. For example, we know that the drug war is a failure. Every reasonable person knows this. Even former U.S. Presidents have now stated that the 40-year War on Drugs has cost far too much for far too little return. That it has drained trillions of dollars from our economy; has caused untold social problems by breaking up the family unit; and has redirected spending away from programs that do work like education and rehabilitation. In 2010, taxpayers paid more than $51 billion to foot the bill for the war on drugs. Moreover, millions of Americans have been incarcerated for low-level drug possession. We need to ask ourselves a pertinent and salient question: how does imprisoning someone for perpetrating a victimless crime, drug use, in the privacy of their home benefit society? Their arrest, trial, and incarceration cost taxpayers close to $50,000 for every year that person is in prison. If that prisoner is the major breadwinner of his/her family, that's another family made dependent on the welfare system. Ultimately, the biggest victim in the incarceration of drug users is the child. With a father or mother or both in jail, their future prospects are made suddenly bleak, which serves only to perpetuate the cycle of poverty. A drug use conviction often leads to a loss of employment, property, food stamp eligibility, financial aid for education, and the right to vote.

Consider that the number of people behind bars for drug violations has risen from 50,000 in 1980 to close to one million today, which represents a nearly 2000 percent increase.

Moreover, more than 80 percent of these arrests were for mere possession, and half of these were for marijuana.

The war on drugs isn't a war on drugs. It's a war on black and brown people. Draconian drugs laws have filled our state prisons with non-violent criminals. Our state prisons are so overcrowded that states have turned to corporations like CCA to build new prisons. Effectively, states have said to corporations, "You front the cash to build the prison, and we will fill it. Then you bill us for the housing of each prisoner." In turn, these for profit prisons say, "If we are going to take the risk of building your prison, then you better enact tough drug laws to ensure we can be sure to fill it." It's hard to think of anything so deplorable than this.

Thankfully, however, some of the more progressive states are awakening to the reality of the futility of fighting this perpetual war, with states like Colorado, Vermont, and Washington decriminalizing pot use. And did you know that in every state or country that has decriminalized drug use, rates of drug addiction and use have fallen, drug crime has plummeted, and the respective government has benefited via increased tax revenues?

But all that follows logic. The opposition of logic comes from the Old Testament inspired Right, and more significantly from the corporations that are invested in prisons. In fact, a read of CCA's corporate documents clearly spells their position on drug enforcement:

> Any changes with respect to drugs and controlled substances or illegal immigration could affect the number of persons arrested, convicted, and sentenced, thereby potentially reducing demand for correctional facilities to house them.

How is this any less morally repugnant than human trafficking? Especially when you consider that the racial and socio-economic biases of the justice system guarantee the disproportionate incarceration of black and brown people. Again, another reason why the Republican Party loves draconian drug laws, because it suppresses the minority vote. Consider that blacks and whites use marijuana at almost identical levels but blacks are four times more likely to be arrested for pot use. Thus the prison system is not only corrupted by for profit interests, it's also corrupted by a political party whose aim is to disenfranchise a segment of the voting population, as a majority of states prohibit people with a criminal record from voting.

Rational people need to fight for changes to not only our drug laws but also the way we think about drug use. In other words, treating drug use as a social problem rather than a criminal problem. Why? Well, we know that way of thinking works. Sure, Portugal isn't a state of America, but their 10-year experience with drug decriminalization is something all democracies should learn from. In 2001, Portugal enacted a nationwide law that decriminalized all drugs, including cocaine and heroin, while drug trafficking remained treated as a criminal offense. It's now been more than a decade since decriminalization began, so what are the results?

The rampant youth drug use and drug tourism that the Portugal far Right predicted never materialized. In fact, drug usage rates in Portugal are now among the lowest in the European Union, and drug-related ills – such as sexually transmitted diseases and deaths due to drug use – have fallen dramatically. And money that was wasted fighting a never-ending drug war has been funneled to successful drug prevention programs, and back into the economy at large.

Corporations are raking in billions of dollars as a result of flawed and failed crime policies, and it's not just the corporations that own the deeds to the prison, it's also ancillary service providers like telecommunication companies. For instance, Sprint, AT&T, and MCI engage in the practice of price gouging when it comes to charging prisoners exorbitant calling charges. In 2012, the city of Chicago realized $3 million in phone call surcharges alone. Like any industry, the name of the game is to squeeze as much profit from every line item or business unit as possible, but pity the non-violent criminal who is serving time for unpaid parking tickets, forced into a private prison whose mission is to cut corners in order to squeeze margins, which ultimately means the prisoner can expect extreme overcrowding, abuses by poorly trained corrections officers, and inadequate food and heating. All the while in the knowledge the prison is not subject to any governmental oversight or scrutiny.

Let's not lose sight of the fact that racial profiling and unconstitutional Stop & Frisk laws are providing a never-ending conveyer belt of minorities for these private prisons. In 2012, New Yorkers were stopped by the police 532,911 times:

- 473,644 were totally innocent (89 percent)
- 284,229 were black (55 percent)
- 165,140 were Latino (32 percent)
- 50,366 were white (10 percent)

And Bill O'Reilly says there's no racism in America today. The above statistics bring to mind the case of George

Zimmerman. Whatever else you think about that trial, one thing is for certain: Zimmerman had pre-determined Trayvon Martin to be up to no good because he was black. Just like the NYPD do every day with Stop & Frisk.

Chris Hedges said, "Poor people, especially those of color, are worth nothing to corporations and private contractors if they are on the streets. In jails and prison, however, they each can generate corporate revenues of $30,000 to $40,000 a year."

Ask yourself this: who is writing criminal law in this country?

While asking yourself that, let's summarize the chapter:

- The Christian Right love draconian criminal punishment laws.
- Corporations profit from draconian criminal punishment laws.
- The Republican Party benefits from draconian criminal punishment laws.

Again, who is writing the laws in this country? And does the answer to that question serve a free democracy? And where are the progressives? We are nowhere. Progressives believe electing a Democrat President solves all problems. It has solved nothing. It solves nothing because our opponents, the far right, are in charge of the hen house, and they are in charge because they are unified, mobilized, and passionate, while we are left to make snarky liberal comments on Twitter. More often than not, progressives are content being the smartest sounding person at a cocktail party. In the era of social media, we think clicking "Like" to a Facebook cause benefits mankind or helps make America better. It doesn't. If you want to stop corporations making insane mountains of money by locking human beings in cages, you need to get active in helping end this drug war. States like Colorado and Washington have led the way, and in 2013 President Obama said the Department of Justice would no longer prosecute pot users in states that have decriminalized marijuana or in states that allow medical marijuana. This is a big step forward, but Obama has made it clear he is only willing to go so far so fast in adjusting the nation's policy towards pot. On the federal level, lasting and meaningful reform, however, will have to come via the Congress, and that's where "we the people" need to make ourselves heard.

CHAPTER NINE
WAR ON THE MIDDLE CLASS

"There's class warfare, all right, but it's my class, the rich class, that's making war, and we're winning."

WARREN BUFFET

The Republican Party has been incredibly effective at marginalizing and sullying the idea of union protection for workers. A 2011 Gallup Poll showed the approval rating for labor unions to be at its lowest level since 1936, with only 52 percent of Americans approving of them. This is remarkable, given 90 percent of Americans believe their personal economic well-being falls somewhere on the scale between lower-middle class to upper-middle class. Moreover, it's difficult to fathom this negativity towards labor unions given it was they who gave us the weekend, fair wages and relative income equality, widespread health coverage, the Medical Leave Act, and helped end child labor.

I get the fact some of you are self-employed, and I get how bureaucratic red tape can be stifling on 'ma and pa' SMEs. I grew up in a small business family and I have owned or part-owned a number of small businesses during my life, so please don't confuse me for being a card carrying teamster. But the facts of the matter are this: when union membership thrives, so does the middle class. And when the middle class thrives, so does the entire American economy. In fact, the decline of union membership mirrors the decline of the middle class. Almost eerily so! Studies by Harvard University, the non-partisan Center for American Progress (CAP), the union-backed Economic Policy Institute (EPI) in Washington, D.C., and the Pew Research Center have shown an irrefutable correlation between the rate of union membership and the percentage of the nation's total wealth held by the middle class. As unions increased their memberships in the years following the Great Depression, the gap between rich and poor narrowed. But as labor unions were weakened by free-trade agreements, globalization, and anti-labor legislation starting in the 1980s, the gap widens to the point of running off the charts.

As union membership rates decrease, middle-class incomes shrink

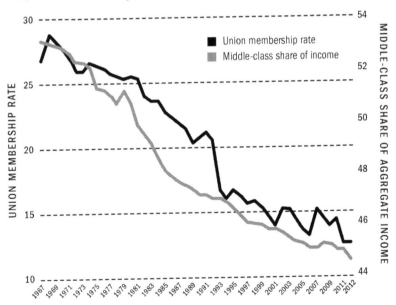

Source: Union membership rate from Barry T. Hirsch, David A. MacPherson, Wayne G. Vroman, "Estimates of Union Density by State", Monthly Labor Review 124 (7) (2001). Middle-class share of aggregate income from U.S. Census Bureau, Current Population Survey (Department of Commerce).

According to the United Nation's 2013 World Happiness Report, the happiest countries on the planet are Denmark, Sweden, The Netherlands, Norway, and Finland. The top 5 share a couple things in common: they like smoked fish that is far too salty, and they have the highest rates of union membership in the world. The percentage of the working population that is covered by collective bargaining: Finland (95%), Denmark (74%), Sweden (92%), Norway (77%), and The Netherlands (82%). According to the report, happy people "live longer, are more productive, earn more and are also better citizens." These countries are also ranked in the top 10 by the U.N for having the highest standard of livings, as determined by such markers as rates of crime, social equality, access to education and healthcare, pollution, and teen pregnancy. So, what of the U.S? In terms of happiness, we rank behind Mexico in 17th. In terms of standard of living, there are fourteen countries ranked above us. In terms of labor protection laws, the U.S. is ranked third last out of 20 OECD countries. The percentage of the labor force that is covered by collective bargaining laws is less than 10 percent. Any questions?

If the experience of Northern Europe is a little too abstract for your liking, then consider the Center for American Progress Action Fund (CAPAF) analysis of Census data, which shows the middle class brings home a substantially larger share of aggregate earnings in states that have high rates of union membership than in those where fewer workers are organized.

From the moment President Reagan declared war on the unions in the summer of 1981, when he fired 13,000 striking air traffic controllers and effectively destroyed their union, America has seen practically all its economic gains go to the top 1 percent. As *Washington Post* columnist Harold Meyerson noted, that was "an unambiguous signal that employers need feel little or no obligation to their workers, and employers got that message loud and clear – illegally firing workers who sought to unionize, replacing permanent employees who could collect benefits with temps who could not, shipping factories and jobs abroad." In 1980, union membership equaled roughly one-third (28 percent) of the work force. At that same time, the middle class claimed more than half of the nation's income (53.2 percent). Today, union membership has plummeted to 10 per cent, while the middle-class share of income has fallen to 46 percent. Conversely, in that same period, the top 1 percent has seen its share of the nation's income soar from 9 percent to 25 percent. While the middle class is struggling to maintain its standard of living, CEO salaries are sky-rocketing. The real spending power of the average worker salary has not increased since the 1970s.

Today, our corporations are the richest in the world. Think about that while you think about this: of the 25 wealthiest countries, the dollar value of the U.S. minimum hourly wage ranks 24th. Why? Well the Christian Right alongside libertarians alongside the Republican Party have dedicated much of the past three decades to destroying the unions. As union membership declined, corporations became free to obliterate wages. And obliterate they did!

In the four decades that followed FDR's New Deal, America built the healthiest middle class in the world. Unions and worker protection laws ensured everyone was paid a higher wage and a comparatively better standard of living. Why? It meant skilled workers and those prepared to work the hardest rarely considered non-union supported jobs. Union protected jobs meant a better wage and benefits. Thus, non-union employers had to compete with the union companies, which meant wages were raised across the board. But we bought into the trickle down bullshit, that corporations are delicate flowers and if we give them every tax cut and regulatory free pass they demand, then the jobs will flow from some eternal spigot.

Today, the "job creators" are threatening to cut jobs if the minimum wage is raised to the $10.15 per hour that President Obama has called for. It's a fundamental economic myth that lower wages creates more jobs for the overall economy. When you raise the minimum wage, the middle class has more to spend. When the middle class spends more, corporations need to hire more to meet the demand. Conversely, when the minimum wage is low, and it's at a 40-year low today, the middle class doesn't spend, which results in corporations sitting on their cash reserves. Today, corporations are sitting on close to $3 trillion profit, while the middle class continues to shrink smaller.

So, how have we let this income disparity happen?

It's happened because the Christian Right believes they truly are millionaires in waiting. They truly believe that any day now, it will be their turn for Jesus to shine his pot of gold upon them. Further, their worship of their second favorite Jesus, Reagan, makes them despise anything that has to do with government intervention or organized labor, even if it's to their economic advantage. The Right has successfully turned neighbor against neighbor, and worker against worker. We are fighting each other rather than against the social injustices that have befallen the country due to big corporations.

In Wisconsin, the Christian Right, with the backing of the Koch brothers, swept Tea Party Governor Scott Walker into office. Walker, the son of a Baptist preacher and a fundamentalist Christian, said in a talk to the Christian Businessmen's Committee, "I follow orders from the Lord. The way to be complete in life is to fully and unconditionally turn your life over to Christ as your personal lord and savior and to make sure that every step of every day is one that you trust and obey, and keep looking out to the horizon to the path that Christ is calling you to follow and know that ultimately he's going to take you home both here at home and ultimately far beyond." He also said God told him when to propose marriage, and when to run for Governor.

His campaign message mirrored the message of the Republican Party: that the economic downturn had nothing to with Wall Street gone wild, and everything to do with union labor and local budget debts and deficits. In other words, the true class conflict the mainstream media never talks about. On one side you have the right-wing billionaires like the Koch brothers; on the other side you have teachers, cops, administrative workers, and janitors. In Wisconsin, Walker's goal was to reduce public-sector unions to the same subjugated state as their counterparts in the private sector, and he is winning. In 2011, Governor Walker signed a law that allowed state and local public employees to opt out of paying dues into public unions. Its genius lies in the fact that when workers have to physically pay for union membership out of their own wallet, rather than have it deducted from their pay, it gives the perception of costing more, which leads to workers dropping their membership. In 2011, membership at Wisconsin's American Federation of State, County and Municipal Employees Council 40 – one of four branches in the state – equaled 31,730 members. By 2013, membership had fallen to just 20,488, which represents a 35 percent decline in membership since Walker's law was enacted. But as MSNBC host Rachel Maddow points out, the Republican economic blueprint has nothing to with balancing budgets (Dick Cheney said, "Deficits don't matter"), and everything to do with controlling political power for their corporate masters:

> The longer it goes on, the clearer it becomes that this whole fight is not about what they say it is about. This whole fight is not about the budget. This fight is about destroying the unions. It is about corporate titans who give lots of money to Republicans and who can get them on the phone for 20 minutes in the middle of a crisis, guys like David Koch wanting to bust the unions, and it is about dismantling a key part of the Democratic base in terms of fund raising. You want to see those numbers from the 2010 elections again? Right. Ok, unions are the only significant outside spending group that Democrats have to compete with the conservatives. Union members also tend to support Democratic causes and they provide a good chunk of the get out the vote infrastructure that Democrats rely on to win elections. The Republican Party more than almost anything else represents corporate interest. The Democratic Party more than anything else represents people who work for corporate interests or people who represent something other than corporations.

To underscore this point, of the top 10 "outside group" electoral campaign spenders in America today, seven are right wing groups, including the Koch Brother's Americans For Prosperity, Karl Rove's Crossroads, and the Chamber of Commerce. The three left wing groups are unions, including the Public Employee Union, and the SEIU. Ok, let's look at the power differential again: it's 7 to 3. Now, if the billionaire-backed Republican Party can completely destroy the unions, then there will be no progressive or left leaning group among the top 10 political spenders in this country. And you think the income gap is wide now? Well, just wait!

So what of Wisconsin today? Walker's state now ranks 49 out of 50 states when it comes to job creation, with an actual decline of 15,900 jobs since he took office in January 2011. And like just about all states that have enacted so-called "right-to-work" legislation, Wisconsin's per capita income has fallen. In fact, the University of New Mexico's Bureau of Business and Economic Research found that 21 of the 23 right-to-work states have per capita incomes below the 2011 U.S. average of $41,600 per year.

From the lone star state to the Appalachians, Republican lawmakers are waging war on union labor. They're passing bills to eliminate collective bargaining all together, or they're writing laws that allow workers to opt-out, like Walker's law in Wisconsin. All in all, this is one of the largest and most focused efforts to destroy American unions in modern times.

Ultimately, we (liberals) are allowing this to happen. We are simply not in the game like our ideological opponents. While they are freely playing the game of class warfare, the one where the rich take from the poor, we are hesitant to fight on equal terms. John Cassidy of *The New Yorker* writes, "Americans are famously reluctant to adopt the language of class warfare, or even to acknowledge its existence. In its place, they have embraced the argot and imagery of individualism: the hardy frontiersman loading his family and his possessions into a single wagon; the industrious immigrant tending his grocery store or gas station 16 hours a day; the spotty post-adolescent hunched over his laptop trying to create the next Facebook." The rich are playing a game so effective that they've succeeded in turning worker against worker. Rarely are the big corporations, in particular Wall Street, indicted for causing the dire economic circumstances the nation finds itself in today. It's always complaints about "union bosses", "jobs for life", and "bloated city pensions".

Ironically, the working class had nothing to do with blowing up the universe. The cause of our economic malaise was the 30-years of financial deregulation and the war on the unions that preceded the eventual crash in 2007. But with one half of the country getting their information from a passive mainstream media, and the other half from the right-wing echo chamber, the poor ("moochers"), and organized labor have been saddled with the sins of the rich. Put another way, the poor and the unions, who represent the middle class, have been framed.

Wall Street's hold on the American economy is so vice-like and its political influence so great that, since 2009, 95 percent of all income gains have gone to the top 1percent, which makes Obama, ironically, the greatest "Republican" president of all time. Of course, finance reform laws must come via the House, and Obama enjoyed a Democratic controlled legislative chamber for a mere two years of his presidency. Ultimately, the financial system is rigged against us. Wall Street, as we know it, is an instrument of class warfare that poses a mortal threat to the middle class and our democratic values.

Wall Street is to today what the East Indies Trading Company was to the 17th century. For the sake of the Founding Fathers' ideals, and the democratic and egalitarian ideals a majority of Americans cherish, we must do what we can to elect candidates like Elisabeth Warren. Candidates who don't subscribe to the doctrine of "too big to fail". Candidates who know that wealth concentrated exclusively at the top is not only a threat to democracy but also to the American way of life.

CHAPTER TEN
THE WAR ON WOMEN

"And, you know, politics aside, the success of Sarah Palin and women like her is good for all women – except, of course, those who will end up, you know, like, paying for their own rape kit 'n' stuff. But for everybody else, it's a win. Unless you're a gay woman who wants to marry your partner of 20 years – whatever. But for most women, the success of conservative women is good for all of us. Unless you believe in evolution. You know – actually, I take it back. The whole thing's a disaster."

TINA FEY

With the make-up of the Republican Party looking more and more like that of the Democratic Party in the 1980s – an umbrella of warring factions – there's seemingly only two things that really unites the entire GOP caucus these days: an insatiable hatred of Obama and the determination of what a woman can and can't do with her own body. While the GOP House cannot pass a single jobs bill, it can pass a bill to ban all post-22 week abortions, even in the knowledge it had no chance of surviving a vote in the Senate. In fact, in 2013 there were nearly 150 abortion bills slated for a vote in state legislatures across America. Arkansas and North Dakota passed laws abortion laws that fly in the face of Roe v Wade. In other words, they passed laws that are brazenly unconstitutional, and despite the

12-hour filibuster effort of instant national women's rights superstar Wendy Davis, Texas passed a bill to ban post-20 week abortions.

Elizabeth Nash, a policy analyst for the Guttmacher Institute, a research group that supports access to abortions, says, "These laws are flying through. The attention has really been at the state level around abortion issues. Now what you also see as the federal is very disturbing, and it shows that abortions opponents are very emboldened."

"Emboldened" means the crazies are coming, and at the expense of everything else that matters, including the economy. For while the economy continues a slow recovery, with stagnant growth numbers, the GOP is putting forward bills on abortion and debates on what does and does not constitute rape, rather than a single piece of legislation to speed up the recovery. So, why do the Republican politicians continue to hammer away on abortion? Because it's a distracting wedge issue. It not only emboldens their base, the Christian Right, it also attracts media attention. And if we are all talking about wedge issues, such as abortion and same-sex marriage, then no one is talking about the real cause of America's problems: the corporate takeover of the nation, and the income disparity and social problems that has caused.

Granted, the notion of a War on Women sounds like partisan hyperbole, but there are many examples from which any fair-minded independent might come to the conclusion that the evidence for an alleged Republican War on Women is conclusive. Moveon.org cited ten examples:

1. Redefining Rape: Not only does the GOP want to reduce women's access to abortion care, they're actually trying to redefine rape.

2. Changing the legal term for victims of rape, stalking, and domestic violence to "accuser," while victims of less gendered crimes, like burglary, remains "victim."

3. In South Dakota, Republicans proposed a bill that could make it legal to murder a doctor who provides abortion care.

4. Republicans want to cut nearly a billion dollars of food and other aid to low-income pregnant women, mothers, babies and kids.

5. In Congress, Republicans have a bill that would let hospitals allow a woman to die rather than perform an abortion necessary to save her life.

6. Maryland Republicans ended all country funding for low-income kids' preschool program. Their argument is women should be at home with the kids, not out working.

7. Congressional Republicans want to cut that same program, Head Start, by $1 billion. This means over 200,000 kids could lose their spots in pre-school.

8. Two-thirds of the elderly poor are women, and Republicans are taking aim at them, too. A spending bill would cut funding for employment services, meals, and housing for senior citizens.

9. Congress voted for a Republican amendment to cut all federal funding from Planned Parenthood health centers, one of the most trusted providers of basic health care and family planning in the country.

10. And if that wasn't enough, Republicans are pushing to eliminate all funds for the only federal family planning program. For humans. But Republican Dan Burton has a bill to provide contraception for wild horses. You can't make this stuff up.

Obviously, these bills have nothing to do with women's health, and everything to do with appeasing religious belief. Moreover, these actions are completely undemocratic given that an overwhelming majority of the national electorate is pro-choice. But there is little doubt that the Republican Party's most holy goal is to deprive women of their reproductive rights and to frame that argument, not as one of health but of religion. To underscore how important war on women is to the GOP's psyche, one only has to realize that of the nearly 40,000 laws of all types enacted in 2011, there were more than 1,000 bills in state legislatures to restrict a woman's right to legal abortion services.

The Guttmacher Institute details the extent of the GOP's war on women's reproductive rights for 2011:

- By almost any measure, issues related to reproductive health and rights at the state level received unprecedented attention in 2011. In the 50 states combined, legislators introduced more than 1,100 reproductive health and rights-related provisions, a sharp increase from the 950 introduced in 2010. By year's end, 135 of these provisions had been enacted in 36 states, an increase from the 89 enacted in 2010 and the 77 enacted in 2009. *(Note: This analysis refers to reproductive health and rights-related "provisions", rather than bills or laws, since bills introduced and eventually enacted in the states contain multiple relevant provisions.)*

- Fully 68 percent of these new provisions – 92 in 24 states – restrict access to abortion services, a striking increase from last year, when 26 percent of new provisions restricted abortion. The 92 new abortion restrictions enacted in 2011 shattered the previous record of 34 adopted in 2005.

- Abortion restrictions took many forms: bans (6 states), waiting periods (3 states), ultrasound (5 states), insurance coverage (3 states joined the existing 5 with such restrictions), clinic regulations (4 states), medication abortion (7 states).

The report goes on to state specific details on the following:

Abortion Restrictions Took Many Forms

Bans. The most high-profile state-level abortion debate of 2011 took place in Mississippi, where voters rejected the ballot initiative that would have legally defined a human embryo as a person "from the moment of fertilization", setting the stage to ban all abortions and, potentially, most hormonal contraceptive methods in the state. Meanwhile, five states (AL, ID, IN, KS and OK) enacted provisions to ban abortion at or beyond 20 weeks' gestation, based on the spurious assertion that a fetus can feel pain at that point. These five states join Nebraska, which adopted a ban on abortions after 20 weeks in 2010.

Waiting Periods. Three states adopted waiting period requirements for a woman seeking an abortion. In the most egregious of the waiting-period provisions, a new South Dakota law would have required a woman to obtain pre-abortion counseling in person at the abortion facility at least 72 hours prior to the procedure; it would also have required her to visit a state-approved crisis pregnancy center during that 72-hour interval. The law was quickly enjoined in federal district court and is not in effect. A new provision in Texas requires that women who live less than 100 miles from an abortion provider obtain counseling in person at the facility at least 24 hours in advance. Finally, new provisions in North Carolina require counseling at least 24 hours prior to the procedure. With the addition of new requirements in Texas and North Carolina, 26 states mandate that a woman seeking an abortion must wait a prescribed period of time between the counseling and the procedure.

Ultrasound. Five states adopted provisions mandating that a woman obtain an ultrasound prior to having an abortion. The two most stringent provisions were adopted in North Carolina and Texas and were immediately enjoined by federal district courts. Both of these restrictions would have required the provider to show and describe the image to the woman. The other three new provisions (in AZ, FL and KS), all of which are in effect, require the abortion provider to offer the woman the opportunity to view the image or listen to a verbal description of it. These new restrictions bring to six the number of states that mandate the performance of an ultrasound prior to an abortion.

Insurance Coverage. Kansas, Nebraska, Oklahoma and Utah adopted provisions prohibiting all insurance policies in the state from covering abortion except in cases of life endangerment; they all permit individuals to purchase additional coverage at their own expense. These new restrictions bring to eight the number of states limiting abortion coverage in all private insurance plans.

These four provisions also apply to coverage purchased through the insurance exchanges that will be established as part of the implementation of health care reform. Five additional states (FL, ID, IN, OH and VA) adopted requirements that apply only to coverage purchased on the exchange. The addition of these nine states brings to 16 the number of states restricting abortion coverage available through state insurance exchanges.

Clinic Regulations. Four states enacted provisions directing the state department of health to issue regulations governing facilities and physicians' offices that provide abortion services. A new provision in Virginia requires a facility providing at least five abortions per month to meet the requirements for a hospital in the state. New requirements in Kansas, Pennsylvania and Utah direct the health agency to develop standards for abortion providers, including requirements for staffing, physical plant, equipment and emergency supplies; supporters of the measures made it clear that the goal was to set standards that would be difficult, if not impossible, for abortion providers to meet. Enforcement of the proposed Kansas regulations has been enjoined by a state court.

Medication Abortion. In 2011, states for the first time moved to limit provision of medication abortion by prohibiting the use of telemedicine. Seven states (AZ, KS, NE, ND, OK, SD and TN) adopted provisions requiring that the physician prescribing the medication be in the same room as the patient.

Family Planning Under Pressure. Family planning services and providers were especially hard-pressed in 2011, facing significant cuts to funding levels, as well as attempts to disqualify some providers for funding because of their association with abortion. Considering the historic fiscal crises facing many states, it is significant that family planning escaped major reductions in nine (CO, CT, DE, IL, KS, MA, ME, NY and PA) of the 18 states where the budget has a specific line-item for family planning. The story, however, was different in the remaining nine states. In six (FL, GA, MI, MN, WA and WI), family planning programs sustained deep cuts, although generally in line with decreases adopted for other health programs. In the other three states, however, the cuts to family planning funding were disproportionate to those to other health programs: Montana eliminated the family planning line item, and New Hampshire and Texas cut funding by 57 percent and 66 percent, respectively.

Indiana, Colorado, Kansas, Ohio, North Carolina Texas and Wisconsin, meanwhile, moved to disqualify or otherwise bar certain types of providers from the receipt of family planning funds. New Hampshire decided not to renew its contract through which the Planned Parenthood affiliate in the state received Title X funds.

Given the difficult fiscal and political climate in states in 2011, it is especially noteworthy that Maryland, Washington and Ohio took steps to expand Medicaid eligibility for family planning. With these changes, 24 states have expanded eligibility for family planning under Medicaid based solely on income; seven have utilized the new authority under health care reform.

Abstinence-Only Education Is Back

Unlike in recent years, when states had moved to expand access to comprehensive, medically accurate sex education, the only relevant measures enacted in 2011 expanded abstinence education. Mississippi, which had long mandated abstinence education, adopted provisions that make it more difficult for a school district to include other subjects, such as contraception, in order to offer a more comprehensive curriculum. A district will now need to get specific permission to do so from the state department of education. A new requirement enacted in North Dakota mandates that the health education provided in the state include information on the benefits of abstinence "until and within marriage". Including North Dakota, 37 states now mandate abstinence education.

The Republican Party's war on women has moved so far to the extreme right that it has prompted the last handful of remaining "moderate" Republicans to sharply criticize their party for focusing on enacting legislation to limit women's access to abortion and contraception. Oklahoma state Representative Doug Cox (R), who also happens to be a physician, said, "What happened to the Republican Party that I joined? The party where conservative presidential candidate Barry Goldwater felt women should have the right to control their own destiny? The party where President Ronald Reagan said a poor person showing up in the emergency room deserved needed treatment regardless of ability to pay? What happened to the Republican Party that felt government should not over regulate people until (as we say in Oklahoma) 'you have walked a mile in their moccasins'? Where did the party go that felt some decisions in a woman's life should be made not by legislators and government, but rather by the women, her conscience, her doctor and her God?"

The GOP continues to offer health policies that are based in superstitious belief. Instead of expanding access to contraception in order to tackle the high rates of unintended teen pregnancy, Republicans are pushing to eliminate Medicaid coverage for Plan B. In state after state, Republican state legislatures are pushing bills through that will force women who opt for an abortion in their first-trimester to undergo the horror of a trans-vaginal ultrasound, because the Christian Right believes abortions are nothing more than a "lifestyle convenience". You see, the party of Christ does not accept that the nightmare a woman goes through when electing for an abortion to be nearly traumatic enough. They demand suffering for your sins, and that's what these trans-vaginal ultrasound bills are designed to do, to make the woman suffer, and it's that kind of language that is written into these laws. For instance, the language of the Wisconsin Senate bill is unapologetic:

> An ultrasound on the pregnant woman using whichever transducer the woman chooses; provide a simultaneous oral explanation during the ultrasound including the number of unborn children and presence and location of the unborn child; display the ultrasound images so that the pregnant woman may view them; provide a medical description of the ultrasound images including the dimensions of the unborn child and a description of any viewable external features and internal organs of the unborn child; and provide a means for the pregnant woman to visualize any fetal heartbeat, in a quality consistent with current medical practice, and a simultaneous oral explanation of the visual display of the heartbeat in a manner understandable to a layperson (ultrasound requirements).

Cruelly and to no one's surprise, these bills make no allowance for victims of rape or incest, so picture a young girl not long out of her teens, who has just experienced the viciousness of rape, and who is now confronted with the emotional cruelty imposed upon her by meaning of this bill.

The nationwide incremental strategy, which has seen Republicans layer anti-abortion bills on top of other anti-abortion bills, is in full earnest since the GOP took control of the Congress and state houses in 2010. If we do nothing to stop this Taliban-like control of our culture, we can expect fewer clinics, and more obstacles for women to deal with their own health issues. Wendy Davis stood for 12 hours without so much as a restroom break to filibuster a bill whose sole purpose is to shut women's health clinics in her home state. In the end she lost that particular battle, but she brought nationwide attention to the Christian fundamentalist takeover of Texas, and as a result she may end up winning the larger war. Ultimately, if Liberals are to prevail, they will need to match Wendy Davis' passion and willingness to fight.

CHAPTER ELEVEN
THE WAR ON PUBLIC EDUCATION

"The school is the last expenditure upon which America should be willing to economize."

FRANKLIN D. ROOSEVELT

Billionaires and corporations have waged a concerted war on public education. In prosecuting this war, they've again found the perfect partner in the Christian Right. Because for biblical literalists, nothing is as Satanic as a math book that claims Pi does not equal exactly 3, or science books that claim early humans didn't keep dinosaurs as pets. Also, they hate that public education has that pesky equal employment opportunity thing. You know, where gays, lesbians, and atheists can be employed as teachers.

For corporations, it's another cornerstone in their agenda to profit from our lives, from the cradle to the grave. Their goal is to channel the middle class away from public schools by promoting their privatized charters. The corporations have not only been successful in shaping public policy, they've also spent millions of dollars in propaganda. They've even funded several films, including *Waiting For Superman*, and *Won't Back Down*. If you haven't seen either documentary, educational historian Diane Ravitch summarized the major themes in an essay published in the *New York Review of Books*:

> American public education is a failed enterprise. The problem is not money. Public schools already spend too much. Test scores are low because there

are so many bad teachers, whose jobs are protected by powerful unions. Students drop out because the schools fail them, but they could accomplish practically anything if they were saved from bad teachers. They would get higher test scores if schools could fire more bad teachers and pay more to good ones. The only hope for the future of our society, especially for poor black and Hispanic children, is escape from public schools, especially to charter schools, which are mostly funded by the government, but controlled by private organizations, many of them operating to make a profit.

Ravitch nails it! Essentially these "documentaries" are little more than a combined four-hour orgy of teacher union bashing. They claim that the entire problem with the public education system boils down to teachers being protected by corrupt unions, while celebrating privatized schools as the ultimate panacea. Presumably, of course, for those kids whose parents can afford it.

Billionaires are ensuring government policy leaves middle class (white) families with no choice but to pay for private tuition fees by ensuring their elected state politicians pass laws to strangle funding to public education. They figure if the schools are made so bad by a lack of teachers, resources, and learning aids, then those who can afford to pay for education, will!

Take North Carolina as an example. That state is virtually the most gerrymandered state in America. Thanks to redistricting, the GOP controls the executive branch and both the senate and the representative assembly for the first time in 150 years. Since 2010, North Carolina has not only launched vicious attacks on abortion rights, voting rights, Medicaid access, and unemployment benefits, it has also made dismantling public education a central component of its mission. In 2013, North Carolina slashed a half-billion dollars in spending on public education. Does that sound bad? It's stupendously bad! Bi-partisan journal *North Carolina Policy Watch* wrote:

> The 2013-15 biennial budget introduces a raft of spending cuts to public schools that will result in no raises for teachers, larger class sizes, fewer teacher assistants, little support for instructional supplies or professional development, and what could amount to the dismantling of the North Carolina Teaching Fellows program. Teachers can say goodbye to tenure and supplemental pay for advanced degrees. As public education tries to provide high quality educational services for all of its students in the face of these severe cuts, lawmakers have simultaneously introduced a "way out" for those who can take advantage: school vouchers.

Ultimately, that's what's at play here. Corporations want to funnel kids away from public schools and towards private for-profit schools, so they can make money from a whole new consumer class, while the Christian Right wants to funnel more kids into religious schools, so that religious indoctrination can continue in the classroom. Parents who cannot afford corporate-owned, private tuition for their children, and for those who wish to raise their kids with secular values, will be left with classrooms with few or inadequate text books; raised class sizes; no teaching assistants; and teachers who are at the bottom of the nation in terms of teacher pay. North Carolina school superintendent June Atkinson noted, "For the first time in my career of more than 30 years in public education, I am truly worried about students in our care."

The North Carolina Association of Educators (NCAE) published a list of the Top 10 Things the North Carolina Legislature Values More than Public Education:

1. Provides a $41,000 tax break to people earning over $1 million per year.

2. Cutting taxes by over $600 million annually focusing on those who make over $250,000 annually while raising taxes on average teachers.

3. Continuing a tax break on yacht sales while requiring teachers to spend more out of their pocket for school supplies.

4. Allowing guns on school grounds.

5. Funding opportunities for unlicensed, underprepared novices to begin teaching with little to no support while discontinuing pay increases for educators who seek masters degrees.

6. Usurping local control of local assets, such as taking a major airport from a major city

7. Suppressing the vote by passing restrictive voter identification programs, limiting voting hours, early voting, eliminating same day registration, and discouraging voter registration of students.

8. Allowing charter schools to expand grade levels without having to seek approval from the State Board of Education.

9. Funding private schools with little-to-no accountability measures in place to protect students and taxpayer funds.

10. Requiring 7th grade teachers to discuss sensitive and scientifically discredited abortion issues with students.

As more and more states become more deeply entrenched with Republican legislatures, more of our nation's kids are denied quality education, which means our kids fall further and further behind the rest of the world, or, more worryingly, our schools become like those in the South. You see, the heavily Christian South stubbornly refuses to support public education. They see it as something that Yankee northerners sought to impose upon the Confederate states. In their book, *Arkansas Politics and Government*, Diane Blair and Jay Barth write, "The common southern view was that education was private, personal, and optional and not public responsibility." This suspicious stubbornness has resulted in the South becoming the intellectual infants of the American experiment. Hey, Skeeter, before you send me an unintelligible "def fret", I have some facts.

According to 2010 U.S. Census estimates, of the 15 states with the lowest high school graduation rates, 11 are in the South. Moreover, not one southern state places in the top 15 for IQ, and only – Virginia – sneaks above the national average. It gets worse. Not a single southern state places in the top 25 for library visits.

A 2006 report by Michael A. McDaniel of Virginia Commonwealth University claimed, "The correlation matrix shows that estimated state IQ has positive correlations with gross state product, state health, and government effectiveness. Estimated state IQ correlated inversely with violent crime. Thus, states with higher estimated state IQ have greater gross state product, citizens with better health, more effective state governments, and less violent crimes."

A further problem is that the government-hating South pays the lowest state property taxes in the country, which further drains public schools of funding. Not one southern state spends above the national average of $12,500 per year, per student.

Enter George W. Bush's infamous No Child Left Behind (NCLB). A law that imposes annual standardized testing with only one objective in mind: to root out schools that are deemed to be "failing" and then turn them into corporate-owned charter schools. Ravitch, who wrote the earlier essay on *Waiting for Superman* and who was also the U.S. Assistant Secretary of Education under George H. Bush, warns that NCLB has set "a timetable for the demolition of public education in the United States." In 2011, the current U.S. Education Secretary Arne Duncan declared that more than 80 percent of American schools are "failing" under the guidelines of NCLB. Chuck Thompson writes, "The countdown will climax in 2014, when virtually all of the country's public schools will meet the legal definition of failure, thus setting them up for the potential private takeover." Thompson also adds that the NCLB law was originally drafted by George W. Bush's Texas cronies and based on specious and now widely discredited achievement statistics of Texas students in the 1990s, and "was specifically designed to erode the power of public schools. The presumed intent was to diminish the role of 'liberal' teachers in modern society and direct the vastly untapped market of private education into the hungry arms of soulless industrialists such as Rupert Murdoch."

Of course, America has a history of using standardized testing to justify a slew of undemocratic measures, including forced segregation of schools and opposition to affirmative action. In 1969, University of California professor Arthur Jensen claimed to have determined that African-American children had lower IQs than white children, and that it was therefore "wasteful to spend educational dollars" on African-American kids.

Effectively, what the privatization of education will accomplish is this: the middle and upper class will enjoy the privilege that comes with privately funded schools, while the poor (largely minorities) will be resigned to a public education system that will be continually starved of funds, under-resourced, and over-populated. It's the cultivation of the underclass, for it cultivates a class of undereducated workers, that provides corporations with an endless supply chain of low pay labor. Ronald Bailey, a former fellow at the W.E.B. Du Bois Institute for African and American research, refers to this political process as "internal colonialism." He writes, "Internal colonialism is nothing more than the domestic face of world imperialism which saw the U.S. and other capitalist countries dominate the world in fulfilling the imperative of capital accumulation through appropriation of the world's human and natural resources. The use of racial minorities brought surpluses to white society that contributed to the growth of monopoly capitalism." In other words, cheap labor led to massive profits for U.S. monopolistic firms, which today have become super-national corporations.

But so long as our corporations are making money, right?

Max Brantley, editor in chief of Little Rock's *Arkansas Times*, says, "What scares me is that it never used to be okay to say you don't care about public schools. Now it's not only okay to say you don't care about public schools, it's okay even to be hostile toward them. Public schools have been the great leveler of America. They were our great achievement. Universal education for all. Now we're ready to give up on all that." Brantley should know, he has reported the decline of the Little Rock school districts for the past 30 years. The decline of public funding for public schools in Arkansas has seen an explosion of private schools and Christian academies. And by "Christian academies" they mean "segregation academies". Today, more than 20 percent of the Little Rock-area students attend one of the city's 39 private schools, up from 6 percent in the 1990s. These predominantly white private schools are free to teach whatever biblically inspired science rubbish they wish, all but ensuring another generation of white supremacist ignoramuses.

Then there is the privatized home schooling movement. Something dreamed up in right wing think tanks with the purpose of training up a generation of cultural warriors to fight the gay, socialist, Muslim, liberal agenda. One former home-schooled student, Ryan Lee Stollar, explained it like this:

> The Christian home school subculture isn't a children first movement. It is, for all intents and purposes, an ideology-first movement. There is a massive, well-oiled machine of ideology that is churning out soldiers for the culture war. Home schooling is both the breeding ground – literally, when you consider the Quiverfull concept – and the training ground for this machinery. I say this as someone who was raised in that world.

Quiverfull is a movement among some conservative evangelical Protestant couples that promotes procreation, and sees children as a blessing from God, thus denying all forms of birth control.

According to the Department of Education, the total home schooling student population has doubled in the past decade, to more than 1.5 million students. Though families opt to home school for a variety of different reasons, the large part of the growth has come from Christian fundamentalism. Most of the curriculum is written by hardcore fundamentalists, and a quick glance at any textbook demonstrates how overtly anti-science it truly is. The Christian Right loves to promote home schooling – Rick Santorum is a huge proponent – because they believe mainstream America is too liberal. They believe every TV show is a subliminal promotional advertisement for the gay lifestyle. A former home schooling parent said:

> There is an atmosphere of real terror among some evangelicals. They are horrified by the fact that Obama is president, and they see the New Atheist movement as a vocal, in your face threat. Plus, they are obsessed with the End Times, and believe that the Apocalypse could happen any day now. They see a demon on every corner. We home schooled because we wanted to protect our children from what we viewed as the total secularization of America. We listened to people like Rush Limbaugh, who told us that America was in the clutches of evil liberal feminist atheists.

More troubling is the authoritarian ideology it promotes. It discourages critical thinking, and leads kids to make poor decisions as it comes to their own sexuality. For girls, it teaches submission to male figures, and that their life's purpose is to be an obedient homemaker. Kathryn Joyce, author of Quiverfull: Inside the Christian Patriarchy Movement writes, "There are families that home school in such a way that education begins to diverge between boys' education and girls' education around the time they hit puberty. Girls stop receiving the same education as their brothers and are trained instead to fulfill the role that they're going to have, which is to be a mother and a submissive wife."

Beyond submission, it's the dissemination of misinformation when it comes to sex education and safe sex. Multiple studies have demonstrated the relationship between the teaching of abstinence only and the high rates of teen pregnancy and sexually transmitted diseases. But if homeschoolers are kept dumb, obedient, and submissive, this suits corporations and the powerbrokers of the Republican Party just fine. A new generation of reliable voters has been cultivated. A cache of reliable voters that do not possess the critical thinking faculties to challenge corporate-driven agendas. That only 21percent of Iowa Republican voters accept climate change is enough data to underscore that point.

So, what of America's intellectual future? When you consider that whites will cease to be the demographic majority by the year 2050, and you consider that the destruction of the public school system is a nefarious attempt to re-segregate our schools, with minorities pushed into the neglected public school system, and you consider that increasingly large swathes of white kids are being channeled towards schools that deny climate change and evolution, then our future is terrifyingly bleak.

CHAPTER TWELVE

THEY WANT YOU DUMB

"He's a man [George W. Bush] who is lucky to be Governor of Texas. He is a man who is unusually incurious, abnormally unintelligent, amazingly inarticulate, fantastically uncultured, extraordinarily uneducated, and apparently quite proud of all these things."

CHRISTOPHER HITCHENS

In his book *Amusing Ourselves to Death*, the late Neil Postman wrote, "Americans are the best entertained and quite likely the least well-informed people in the Western world." I believe Postman was a little too kind. I would argue that this generation of Americans is the dumbest and least intellectually inquisitive the Western hemisphere has ever seen, and I include Tasmania, Australia. But our collective dumbness is just the way the corporate elite would like us. You see, the goal of anti-intellectualism is to oppress political dissent and, in the Christian Right, corporate interests have again found the perfect partner to help them in their goal of cutting taxes, opposing green initiatives, expanding oil drilling, increasing military spending, and eliminating benefits for the working class.

Now that the Christian Right has seized control of the Republican Party, up is down, and down is up. Black is white, and greenhouse gases are good for the environment. In fact, intellectualism, thinking, and facts are sneered at as if they were a pedophile moving into the apartment next door. Nobel Laureate economist Paul Krugman wrote, "Know-nothingism – the insistence that there are simple, brute-force, instant-gratification answers to every problem, and that there's something effeminate and weak about anyone who suggest otherwise – has become the core of Republican policy and political strategy. The party's de facto slogan has become: 'Real men don't think things through'."

The GOP's primary process to choose its nominee for the 2012 election revealed to the world just how far the party had been pulled to the right by religious conservatives, as the party base and its leaders openly mocked education, and successfully turned "intellectual" into a generic slur. In fact, GOP presidential hopeful Rick Santorum, who would only later lose the nomination to Romney because of a lack of cash, called President Obama a "snob" for saying he wanted all Americans to have access to college.

The collective policy announcements of the 2012 GOP contenders amounted to, in terms of substance, a race to the intellectual bottom. Absent details, facts, and independent enquiry, the candidate's respective hashed out social and economic policies were no more than emotion-driven bumper stickers, and at complete odds with reality. Pizza delivery CEO Herman Cain called for a 9-9-9 tax, which would only reward those at the top, while punishing everyone else in the middle and at the bottom, and would fail to balance a budget. Michele Bachmann said the HPV vaccination causes "mental retardation". It does not! Newt Gingrich's solution to immigration is a double electrified fence on the Mexican border. Rick Perry said he'd get rid of three government departments but could only name two of them. When asked how he'd handle foreign policy better than Obama, the Texas Governor criticized the President, "Well, I wouldn't try to outsmart everyone in the room." Ron Paul said we can solve all of America's problems by getting rid of every single federal government institution. What he would suddenly do with nearly 5 million government employees he didn't say. Nor did he answer how, in turning all power back to the States, he would be able to stop Republican controlled states reenacting Jim Crow laws and establishing laws to award the death penalty to doctors that perform abortions. Newt Gingrich's solution to high levels of black teen unemployment was to make them janitors.

The only true moderate Conservative in the GOP race was former ambassador to China Jon Huntsman, who mocked his fellow candidates, "To be clear, I believe in evolution and trust scientists on global warming. Call me crazy." So, while Huntsman cast a lonely figure when it came to climate change and evolution, let's see what his Republican opponents had to say:

- **Michele Bachmann:** "Carbon dioxide is not a harmful gas; it is a harmless gas... And yet we're being told that we have to reduce this natural substance and reduce the American standard of living to create an arbitrary reduction in something that is naturally occurring in the Earth."

- **Herman Cain:** "I don't believe... global warming is real. Do we have climate change? Yes. Is it a crisis? No. ... Because the science, the real science, doesn't say that we have any major crisis or threat when it comes to climate change."

179

- **Ron Paul:** "While it is evident that the human right to produce and use energy does not extend to activities that actually endanger the climate of the Earth upon which we all depend, bogus claims about climate dangers should not be used as a justification to further limit the American people's freedom."

- **Rick Perry:** "I think there are a substantial number of scientists who have manipulated data so that they will have dollars rolling in to their projects. I think we're seeing it almost weekly or even daily, scientists who are coming forward and questioning the original idea that man-made global warming is what is causing the climate to change."

- **Mitt Romney:** "Do I think the world's getting hotter? Yeah, I don't know that, but I think that it is. I don't know if it's mostly caused by humans...What I'm not willing to do is spend trillions of dollars on something I don't know the answer to."

- **Rick Santorum:** "I believe the earth gets warmer and I also believe the earth gets cooler. And I think history points out that it does that and that the idea that man, through the production of CO_2 — which is a trace gas in the atmosphere, and the man-made part of that trace gas is itself a trace gas — is somehow responsible for climate change is, I think, just patently absurd when you consider all the other factors, El Niño, La Niña, sunspots, moisture in the air ... To me, this is an opportunity for the left to create — it's really a beautifully concocted scheme because they know that the earth is gonna cool and warm."

On evolution, the candidates had this to say during the campaign:

- **Michele Bachmann:** "I support intelligent design. What I support is putting all science on the table and then letting students decide. I don't think it's a good idea for government to come down on one side of scientific issue or another, when there is reasonable doubt on both sides."

- **Ron Paul:** "I think there is a theory, a theory of evolution, and I don't accept it. ... The creator that I know created us, each and every one of us and created the universe, and the precise time and manner ... I just don't think we're at the point where anybody has absolute proof on either side."

- **Rick Perry:** "I am a firm believer in intelligent design as a matter of faith and intellect, and I believe it should be presented in schools alongside the theories of evolution."

- **Mitt Romney:** "I'm not exactly sure what is meant by intelligent design. But I believe God is intelligent, and I believe he designed the creation. And I believe he used the process of evolution to create the human body ... True science and true religion are on exactly the same page. They may come from different angles, but they reach the same conclusion. I've never found a conflict between the science of evolution and the belief that God created the universe. He uses scientific tools to do his work."

- **Rick Santorum:** "I believe in Genesis 1:1 — God created the heavens and the earth ... If Gov.

Huntsman wants to believe that he is the descendant of a monkey, then he has the right to believe that — but I disagree with him on this and the many other liberal beliefs he shares with Democrats. For Jon Huntsman to categorize anyone as 'anti-science' or 'extreme' because they believe in God is ridiculous."

Now, these are the leaders of the Republican Party appealing to the base – the Christian Right, so imagine how much further the rank and file of the GOP are from accepting science and fact. You get people like Delaware Senate hopeful Christine O'Donnell who said, "If evolution is real, how come there are still monkeys?" Well, Christine, education is real, and there are still morons.

Now, the purpose of this chapter is to not argue the merits of evolution or climate change, because if you don't accept both, then you probably wouldn't be reading this book. Also, I'm not a scientist, so I will leave it to the "snobs" as Rick Santorum calls them, or professors as I call them, to explain the robustness of scientific rigor. The objective is to show how the anti-rationalism and anti-intellectualism of the Christian Right, the core of the Republican Party, is fostered and encouraged because not only does it suit the interests of corporations, but it also poses an indelible threat to our democracy. Typically I steer away from the far left as much as I like to drive over the top of the far right, in my truck, but left wing radio talk show host Mike Papatonio got it right when he said, "Anti-intellectualism and anti-rationalism have become almost epidemic in America. Chances are, if you are one of those corporate media-following bone heads who still believe that weapons of mass destruction were found in Iraq, or Saddam Hussein blew up in the Twin Towers, or

Obama is a secret Muslim, or Obama wants to take away your guns, or Obama has FEMA prison camps set up for Teabag Republicans, then search no further. You truly are the under-educated, child-like, impressionable, irrational, dangerous cog in America's political system that puts democracy at risk."

The biggest single mistake liberals make is to presume the leaders of the Republican Party are as stupid as the "red meat to the base" remarks they make. Even today, liberals love making jokes about the presumed intellectual retardation of George W. Bush. Ok, I admit it, I love doing that, too! What lazy joke writer doesn't, right? But the fact is he was far from being the dummy we progressives portrayed him to be. For goodness sake, he graduated from Yale, which is something that many of us who poke fun at his lack of intellect couldn't have done (because we don't have mega-rich parents, but I digress). The point is, politicians on the right use folksiness as a major component of their political strategy. The "Aww, shucks I'm just as undereducated as you" is straight out of the political playbook identity politics 101. It's nothing more than a political illusion that serves their purpose, which is to marginalize the educated elite who typically lean progressive. It's meant to stigmatize scientists and high falutin economists so serving as a weapon in countering facts that run counter to their political self-serving arguments and policies. The then candidate G.W. Bush used this tactic beautifully against Vice President Gore during the 2000 presidential debates, and it is a tactic that Republicans have used successfully against their more intellectual sounding opponents for more than a generation. In his book *The Political Mind*, Drew Westen cites a number of specific examples whereby a Republican has defeated facts and logic by marginalizing intellect and appealing to emotion. When moderator Jim Leher turned the debate to Medicare, the candidates entered the following exchange:

Gore: Under the Governor's plan, if you kept the same fee for service that you now have under Medicare, your premiums would go up by between 18 percent and 47 percent, and that is the study of the Congressional plan that he's modeled his proposal on by the Medicare actuaries. Let me give you one quick example. There is a man here tonight named George McKinney from Milwaukee. He's 70 years old, has high blood pressure, his wife has heart trouble. They have an income of $25,000 a year. They can't pay for their prescription drugs. Under my plan, half of their costs would be paid right away. Under Governor Bush's plan, they would get not one penny for four to five years and then they would be forced to go into an HMO or to an insurance company and ask them for coverage, but there would be no limit on the premiums or the deductibles or any of the terms and conditions.

Bush: I cannot let this go by, the old-style Washington politics, if we're going to scare you in the voting booth. Under my plan the man gets immediate help with prescription drugs. It's called Immediate Helping Hand. Instead of squabbling and finger pointing, he gets immediate help. Let me say something.

Moderator: You're –

Gore: They get $25,000 a year income; that makes them ineligible.

Bush: Look, this is a man who has great numbers. He talks about numbers. I'm beginning to think not only did he invent the internet, but he invented the calculator. It's fuzzy math.

How big was *that* moment in the debate? Well, many pundits believe that was the moment that won Bush the presidency (if you don't count the fact he lost the popular vote and you discard the Supreme Court's intervention). In one simple folksy sentence, "It's fuzzy math," Bush was able to portray Gore as an emotionless policy wonk – "not a regular guy, like us." And the Christian Right loves nothing more than a regular guy (evangelical Christian), especially one who appears in their own image. As a result, uninsured Christians earning not much more than $25,000 per year clamored over each other to vote for Bush, even though he was the candidate whose healthcare policy did not favor their interests.

This crass manipulation of reality plays into the economic despair of the Republican base for it lays the blame for economic malaise at the feet of intellectuals, liberals, minorities, gays and the poor. It paints government as the problem, and corporations as the persecuted saviors of all. This corporate sponsored and orchestrated dumbing down of America is no different than the tactics employed by any number of totalitarian regimes in the past. Hitler's populist rhetoric featured anti-intellectualism, as did his political polemic, *Mein Kampf*. Under Pol Pot, academics were the first to be slaughtered in the Killing Fields. In short, dictatorships don't like smart people. And nor do the CEOs at the helm of America's largest companies, because a smart electorate would never allow passage of a bill that would cut Environmental Protection Authority control and allow for an increase of 42 million more tons of pollution emitted to be called, cynically, the Clear Skies Initiative. Anti-intellectualism allows Republicans who favor tax breaks for the wealthy elite to curry favor with lower and middle-class voters, and these fertile grounds for the rich are plowed on the back of religion in this country. Susan Jacoby, in *The Age of American Unreason*, writes, "One of the most powerful taboos in American life concerns speaking ill of anyone else's faith – an injunction rooted in confusion over the difference between freedom of religion and granting religion immunity from the critical scrutiny applied to other social institutions. Both the Constitution and the pragmatic realities of living in a pluralistic society enjoin us to respect our fellow citizen's right to believe whatever they want – as long as their belief, in Jefferson's phrase, 'neither picks my pocket nor breaks my leg.' But many Americans have misinterpreted this sensible laissez-faire principle to mean that respect must be accorded the beliefs themselves. This mindless tolerance, which places observable scientific fact, subject to proof, on the same level as improvable supernatural fantasy, has played a major role in the resurgence of both anti-intellectualism and anti-rationalism."

One has to ask the obvious question, in what intellectual society would John McCain get away with choosing Sarah Palin, who believes the Queen is the leader of England, and evolution and climate to be the propaganda of the "lamestream" gay secular liberal agenda, to be the Vice President of the nation? Not only did John McCain get away with it, his Veep pick got him into the race. In fact, Palin's nomination turned a 10-point deficit into a 2-point lead in some polls in the weeks leading up to election day.

Jacoby makes the point that we have become so anti-intellectual that we are unable to deal successfully with the complex and dynamic circumstances we face as a society. For instance, American 15-year-olds rank 24th out of 29 countries in math literacy, and their parents are as likely to believe in flying saucers as in evolution. This would be funny if it weren't so serious. According to the Program on International Policy Attitudes at the University of Maryland, in the 2004 election, nearly 70 percent of Bush voters believed the United States had "clear evidence" that Saddam Hussein was working closely with Al Qaeda; a third believed WMDs were found in Iraq; and more than a third believed that a substantial majority of world opinion supported the U.S. led invasion. Clearly, agenda-driven misinformation is the tool to drive the base of the Republican Party, and that's something that's not too hard to accomplish when the base, the Christian Right, distrusts science, facts, intellectuals, and books as much as they do. Stephen Colbert mocked, "I don't trust books. They're all fact, no heart. And that's exactly what's pulling our country apart today. Because face it, folks, we are a divided nation. Not between Democrats or Republicans, or conservatives and liberals, or tops and bottoms. No, we are divided by those who think with their head, and those who know with their heart."

Chris Mooney, author of *The Republican War on Science and Unscientific America*, says the Republican Party move towards anti-intellectualism began in the 1960s. "The Republican political elites decided to energize their base around cultural war issues, like women's rights, gay rights, separation of church and state, and abortion. It was called 'Nixon's Southern Strategy', and it worked: the Republicans became the party of people who have very, very traditionalists views on cultural issues."

This Nixonian strategy actually changed conservative psychology, according to Mooney. "It's been argued convincingly that when you energize people around these sort of issues you get an authoritarian streak coming out, characterized by rigidity and inflexibility, thinking that you're absolutely right and the other side is absolutely wrong; a need for certainty, a need for order." Of course, this type of rigidity does not align itself well with scientific enquiry and with voters who value critical thought. As a result, the party has pushed away people with advanced degrees and expertise. "The more the Republican Party rejects nuance and attacks knowledge, the more the people who have knowledge go the other way. It shows in statistics about liberalism among professors and scientists, and distribution of PhDs across the parties: there's a giant knowledge and expertise gap."

Thanks to the Christian Right, the nation has become an intellectual two-speed nation, with an informed and technocratic elite on one side, and a willfully and proudly ignorant mass on the other. The problem for us all is the stupid party has figured out how to win elections, albeit disingenuously, and that is a giant threat to the future of America.

CHAPTER THIRTEEN

ISRAEL AND THE ROAD TO ARMAGEDDON

"Let me tell you what the Cain Doctrine would be, as it relates to Israel if I were president. You mess with Israel, you are messing with the United States of America!"

HERMAN CAIN

Arguably, the most perverse political relationship of expediency is that between the Christian Right and the state of Israel. For Israel, the American brand of Christianity is its most strategic military asset, its ultimate defense shield. For the Christian Right, Israel represents the final pivot point in ensuring the Bible's blueprint for the end-times unfolds. In fact, biblical end time's theology has it that the world will experience a period of worsening tribulations until the emergence of the Second Coming of Christ.

The Bible claims that Christ returns to earth in fulfillment of his prophecies and to fulfill the prophecies made about him. It is the event when Jesus Christ returns to the earth to defeat evil and establish His reign of justice and peace for the next 1,000 years. During his Millennial Reign he will rule the world from atop Zion (the place now occupied by Mt. Moriah) in Jerusalem. Preceding the establishment of Christ's reign is the Rapture, whereby already deceased Christians emerge from their graves with their eternal bodies to meet Jesus in heaven. The then living

Christians do likewise, and room is made for 144,000 converted Jews who are living in Israel at that time. The unconverted Jewish population of Israel, the 7.5 million that will be left behind, are exterminated at Armageddon, which refers to a town called Megiddo in Northern Israel. This explains the Christian Right's love for Israel. Now in case you missed it the first time, Christian America supports Israel because it means clearing a place for them to meet Jesus, so the Jews can eventually be exterminated.

So, why does Israel love the Christian Right? Well, like everything else broken in our democracy, it comes down to cash. You see, Israel is the largest beneficiary of U.S. financial aid, receiving more than $3 billion each year. More startling is the fact that Israel has a developed economy, and is the only developed nation among the top 10 recipients. What makes this level of direct aid even more extraordinary is the fact that $3 billion equals more than $500 per year for each Israeli. It gets worse. Unlike every single other foreign recipient of our tax dollars, Israel gets their aid in one lump payment at the start of each financial year, whereas other nations receive theirs in quarterly payments. This allows Israel to accumulate interest on the unspent portion. The Congressional Research Service (CRS) estimates that it costs U.S. taxpayers more than $60 million per year to borrow the funds for the early lump sum payment and, according to the U.S. Embassy in Israel, the early transfer of funds has allowed Israel to earn more than $600 million in interest since 2004. Further, Israel is offered many other special deals as reward for our "special relationship", including the fact that Israel is the only beneficiary of U.S. aid that does not need to account how it is spent. Loan guarantees are offered to Israel at lower interest rates and, while private donations to most foreign countries are not tax deductible, that rule does not apply to Israel. In fact, former Israeli Prime Minister Shimon Peres revealed in his memoirs that private donations from wealthy Jews in America had helped finance Israel's illegal nuclear program in the 1950s and 1960s.

The Christian Right has formed a plethora of political action groups whose sole purpose is to encourage policy that supports Israel. These groups include Christian United for Israel, the National Christian Leadership for Israel, the Unity Coalition for Israel, Christian Friends of Israeli Communities, the Christian's Israel Public Action Committee, the International Christian Embassy Jerusalem, and a number of smaller coalitions and committees. The Christian Right have so entrenched Israel into the psyche of the Republican Party that many of the seemingly endless 2012 GOP Presidential Primary debates became little more than an Israel love-in fest, with each candidate failing to resist the urge to prove his obsessively pro-Israel credentials.

On the surface, the infatuation with Israel is especially odd given less than 2 percent of American voters are Jewish. But in debate after debate, Israel was a subject of intense focus among the candidates, with Newt Gingrich declaring the Palestinians to be an "invented people". Michele Bachmann used almost mystical language when saying, "Our nation is blessed because of our relationship with Israel." Rick Perry said, "I also as a Christian have a clear directive to support Israel, so from my perspective it's pretty easy, both as an American and as a Christian, I am going to stand with Israel." Newt Gingrich stated that Israel would be his very first priority as president, "In a Gingrich administration, the opening day, there will be an executive order about two hours after the inaugural address. We will send the embassy from Tel Aviv to Jerusalem as of that day." I guess this means that under a Gingrich presidency, America would have to wait in line.

In John J. Mearsheimer's *The Israel Lobby and U.S. Foreign Policy*, the author writes, "Serious candidates for the highest office in the land will go to considerable lengths to express their deep personal commitment to one foreign country – Israel – as well as their determination to maintain unyielding U.S. support for the Jewish state. Each candidate will emphasize that he or she fully appreciates the multitude of threats facing Israel and make it clear that, if elected, the United States will remain firmly committed to defending Israel's interests under any circumstances. None of the candidates is likely to criticize Israel in any significant way or suggest that the United States ought to pursue a more even-handed policy in the region."

The question then becomes why does Israel receive such extraordinary deference from America's politicians, particularly on the right? Well, the answer to that is the Christian Right has helped make the Israel lobby the most powerful interest group in the United States. So much so that it has become a Republican Party rite of passage for a politician to fly to Israel to receive the blessing of the Israeli Prime Minister. On his trip to Israel during the 2012 campaign, Mitt Romney said, "I would treat Israel like the friend and ally it is… I cannot imagine going to the United Nations, as Obama did, and criticizing Israel in front of the world. You don't criticize your allies in public to achieve the applause of your foes. If there were places where we disagree, I would hold these disagreements in private conversations, not in public forums."

Romney's professed unconditional infatuation led Israeli Prime Minister Benjamin Netanyahu to break protocol, the one that says an ally should never endorse a candidate against an incumbent U.S. president, by endorsing Romney. Following the candidate's visit, a GOP political TV advertisement featuring Netanyahu and the slogan, "The world needs American strength, not apologies", made its way to the airwaves. The Israel newspaper *Ha-aretz* wrote, "In general, Netanyahu embraced Romney as no Israeli prime minister has ever before embraced a candidate running against an incumbent U.S. president: aside from their working meeting in the morning, Netanyahu also hosted Romney and his wife and sons for dinner at his official residence."

The Israel lobby helps shape not only presidential elections, but also congressional, gubernatorial, and senate races. The most pro-Israel candidates attract the most money. Likewise, those who are critical of Israel policy can expect their direct political opponent to receive prompt and sizeable campaign donations. The influence of Israel in our policy decisions is a threat to our democracy because these decisions don't often reflect the will of the people. In a 2006 survey of international relations scholars in the United States, 66 percent of the respondents said that they agreed with the statement "Israel has too much influence on U.S. policy." A national poll showed that 39 percent of respondents said that they believe that the "work of the Israel lobby on Congress and the Bush administration was a key factor for going to war in Iraq and now confronting Iran." Considering I'd guess that 50 percent of America has never heard of the Israel lobby, that's a remarkable result. Not only does the influence of the Christian Right and the Israel lobby lead us to making a great number of decisions that are counter to our national interests, but, as Mearsheimer says, it puts us on the back foot in fighting the War on Terror:

> Washington's close relationship with Jerusalem makes it harder, not easier, to defeat the terrorists who are now targeting the United States, and it simultaneously undermines America's standing with important allies around the world. Now that the Cold War is over, Israel has become a strategic liability for the United States. Yet, no aspiring politician is going to say so in public, or even raise the possibility.

Not only is our uneven handed approach in dealing with Israel hurting our ability to fight terrorism, but one can argue that it's this relationship that is the sole igniter of terrorist acts committed against us and is harmful to our national interest when it comes to foreign policy overall. For instance, in the months that followed 9/11, the Iranian government reached out to the U.S. with the purpose of establishing closer ties. In fact, much of the pre-war intelligence we gained on the Taliban came directly from Tehran. But Israel, via its proxy the Israel lobby, lobbied hard to ensure any détente between the U.S. and Iran would never become a reality. The lobby's efforts to scuttle the fledgling relationship have served only to strengthen Iran's hard-liners, which only serve to make Israel's security problems and ours more difficult. So how does our Christian Right-driven relationship with the Jewish state benefit our foreign policy interests, given that the overriding goal of U.S. foreign policy is to ensure the safety and prosperity of the American people?

There is a case to be made that a strong Israel serves the nation's interests because it's the only genuinely democratic state in the Middle East. Israel's military and political importance in the Middle East and its strategic position stabilize the entire area. Including the oil fields of the Persian Gulf. During the Cold War, Israel curtailed the Soviet Union's expansionist ambitions in the region. Today, it's a western bulwark against the aggressive intents of Iran and other Arab/Persian states. But these benefits have been long established, and now Israel is a nuclear weapon state with one of the most sophisticated military machines in the world. It is a rich country, and an established state that is under no threat from any of its neighbors, even collectively. In 1969, Israel defeated the combined might of Egypt, Syria, and Jordan in just six days. In the 40 plus years since that conflict, Israel has moved even further ahead militarily than its neighbors, and since that war the U.S. pays a huge amount of foreign aid to Egypt, which effectively serves as a bribe to not attack Israel. So there is little justification for supporting the idea that the U.S. should be providing as much direct aid to Israel as it does today.

With so many domestic programs being cut from the U.S. budget, and with sequester cuts reducing so many public services that Americans depend upon, it is absurd that many of these come at the expense of providing Israel $3 billion in military aid. The only beneficiary in this equation is the industrial military complex. Of course!

An ideal ending to this chapter is to close with the final comments of John Mearsheimer and StephenWalt's book, *The Israeli Lobby and U.S. Foreign Policy*:

> Israel's creation and subsequent development is a remarkable achievement. Had American Jews not organized on Israel's behalf and convinced important politicians to support their objectives, Israel might never have been established. U.S. and Israeli

interests have never been identical, however, and Israel's current policies are at odds with America's own national interests and certain core U.S. values. Unfortunately, in recent years the lobby's political clout and public relations acumen have discouraged U.S. leaders from pursuing Middle East policies that would advance American interests and protect Israel from its worst mistakes. The lobby's influence, in short, has been bad for both countries.

There is, nonetheless, a silver lining in America's plight. Because of the costs of these failed policies are now so apparent, we have an opportunity for reflection and renewal. Although the lobby remains a powerful political force, its adverse impact is increasingly hard to overlook. A country as rich and powerful as the United States can sustain flawed policies for quite some time, but reality cannot be ignored forever.

What is needed, therefore, is a candid but civilized discussion of the lobby's influence and a more open debate about U.S. interests in this vital region. Israel's well being is one of those interests – on moral grounds – but its continued presence in the Occupied Territories is not. Open debate and more wide-ranging media coverage will reveal the problems that the current "special relationship" creates and encourages the United States to pursue policies in line with its own national interest, with the interests of other states in the region, and, we firmly believe, with Israel's interests as well.

THE ECHO CHAMBER

> **"He sat down for a one-on-one with Fox News. Very bold choice. Dick Cheney sitting down with Fox News is like Mrs. Butterworth sitting down with the Pancake Channel."**
>
> **JIMMY KEMMEL**

During a 1787 British parliamentary debate, Irish statesman Edmund Burke said, "There are Three Estates in Parliament, the Lords Spiritual, the Lords Temporal, and the Commons. But, in the Reporters' Gallery yonder, there sat a Fourth Estate more important far than they all." Thus coining the origin of the media being referred to the "fourth estate". Martin Lee, author of *Unreliable Sources*, writes:

> In United States English, the phrase "fourth estate" is contrasted with the "fourth branch of government", a term that originated because no direct equivalents to the estates of the realm exist in the United States. The "fourth estate" is used to emphasize the independence of the Press, while the "fourth branch" suggests that the Press is not independent of the government.

A well-functioning media is an essential component of a healthy democracy. After all, a free press is what distinguishes a democracy from a dictatorship. Moreover, it's impossible to have a healthy democracy without an informed electorate, otherwise voters will cast their votes based on ignorance or misinformation. Further, the role of the media is, in effect, to "keep the bastards honest". Without information from a free press, the electorate would have no real means of knowing whether or not politicians were keeping true to their oaths of office. Also, there'd be no means for electoral oversight, which is ultimately what protects our democracy against abuses of power.

This is how it used to work, but the build up to the Iraq invasion in 2003 made it clear that there are now only two kinds of media in America today: The mainstream media, which the Right wrongly believes has a liberal agenda; it doesn't! And then there's the propaganda media, including outlets such as Fox News, MSNBC, *Washington Post*, etc.

The mainstream media, CNN, CBS, ABC, NBC, you name it, has no interest in journalism or investigative reporting today. They are ratings-driven infotainment outlets. Consider that at this given moment, as I type the words onto this page, I have CNN on in the background. Now, also consider the fact that there are some highly complex political, economical, and social debates occurring in the public domain today. Bradley Manning is being tried for aiding the enemy; North Carolina is enacting the most blatantly discriminatory voting laws ever seen in America since 1965; a record number of civilians have been killed by sectarian violence in Iraq this month with another 56 people killed in a suicide blast in Baghdad; the GOP Congress is voting to repeal Obamacare for the 40th time and thus wasting more tax payer dollars; fast food workers across the country are protesting against the cruelty of the minimum wage; Edward Snowden continues to be holed up in a Moscow airport; and NSA officials continue to lie about the dynamics of their eavesdropping programs. Yet CNN has spent five minutes covering birth of the world's biggest baby. Ten minutes on, Diane Lane playing Hillary Clinton in a new television movie. Four minutes to Naomi Watts playing Princess Diana in another movie. And another 10 minutes to a petty verbal squabble between Governor Chris Christie and Senator Rand Paul, which ended with the latter making a very un-clever fat joke. Yet no coverage to any of the important issues of the day mentioned.

Even when the mainstream media is reporting the issues central to our democracy, not only are they covering it in a nauseatingly superficial manner but they also do it in a way that panders to the gods of mindless objectivity. Ok, for clarification – journalists should always exhibit a bias towards objectivity. Being objective – dealing with facts without distortion of personal feelings – should always be the goal of journalism. But the mainstream media's desperation to appear unbiased at all times has meant journalists have confused objectivity with neutrality. In their haste to present both sides of the political spectrum, and in their urge to equally highlight inconsistencies on all sides, the mainstream media often presents a false equivalency. In other words, not all political arguments are equally valid. Paul Krugman wrote about this phenomenon, "If a presidential candidate were to declare that the earth is flat, you would be sure to see a news analysis under the headline 'Shape of the Planet: Both Sides Have a Point.' After all, the earth isn't perfectly spherical."

Strategically, the Romney/Ryan 2012 campaign took advantage of the mainstream's reluctance to call out bullshit by launching what was effectively a "Say Anything" campaign to the White House. For example, a slew of independent studies have shown you cannot cut taxes by 20 percent and close enough loopholes to be revenue neutral without raising taxes on the middle class. But Romney/Ryan were able to trot this out as the basis of their economic plan, unchallenged by a media that goes to pains to present both sides of the topic. For instance, we know that 98 percent of the world's climate scientists agree that humans are causing the planet to heat, but the media presents this debate from both sides: climate change deniers versus believers, with each having an equally valid argument. They clearly don't! The independent fact-checker group PolitiFact identified 24 lies told in 40 minutes by Paul Ryan during the vice presidential debate, and the best commentary we got from CNN was Gloria Bergen saying, "I think he played a little fast and loose with some of his statements." Fast and loose? He told one blatant untruth every 90 seconds in what was effectively a national job interview.

That's what our democracy has to contend with on the mainstream wing of the fourth estate. On the other side, we have the vast right wing media. (Let's face it, no one on the left watches MSNBC.) At its center is Fox News, the number one cable news channel in the country, with more than 2.5 million Americans tuning in during prime time hours (7-9pm), while 30 million tune in daily to the racist and misogynistic rants of Rush Limbaugh. Now, despite Fox News being the communication arm of the Republican Party, the network's slogan is "Fair & Balanced". The network justifies its slogan on the premise that the mainstream media has a liberal bias, despite their being no data to support that. In fact, Kathleen Jamieson, author of *Echo Chamber: Rush Limbaugh and the Conservative Establishment*, points out, "Our exploration of the conservative media's indictment of 'liberal media' is set for us in a context in which scholarly efforts to isolate mainstream media bias have largely come up empty. A meta-analysis of 59 studies found no bias in newspapers and measurable but insignificant biases in news magazines and televisions news, with slightly more statements by Republicans in magazines and slightly more by Democrats on television."

If there is a bias in the mainstream media, it is arguably to the right. Eric Alterman, who wrote *What Liberal Media?*, argues that the Fourth Estate is now dominated by the Right. "Conservatives have spent billions to pressure the mainstream media to move rightward and to create their own parallel media structure. Unbeknownst to millions of Americans who continue to believe that the media are genuinely liberal—or that liberals and conservatives are engaged in a fair fight of relative equality—liberals are fighting a near-hopeless battle in which they are enormously outmatched in most measures."

In a 2000 interview in the *New York Observer*, Vice President Al Gore argued that "most of the media have been slow to recognize the pervasive impact of this fifth column in their ranks that is, day after day, injecting the daily Republican talking points into the definition of what's objective as stated by the news media as a whole. Something will start at the Republican National Committee, inside the building, and it will explode the next day on right-wing talk-show network and on Fox News, and in the newspapers that play this game."

The right wing echo chamber that is Fox News, and the radio talk shows of Rush Limbaugh, Michael Savage, Glenn Beck and the likes, allow the Christian Right to inculcate themselves in a protective media space that is absent of dissenting ideas or antagonistic views. More significantly, it allows the economic message of big corporations to gain favor with the Republican base – middle class evangelicals. After all, you're never going to hear the world's leading economists demonstrate trickle down economics to be a proven myth on Fox & Friends. You will have to read that in the *New York Times*. If you're lucky!

In an environment of unchallenged hyper-partisan rhetoric, the loudest voices become the ones most heard. And the loudest are generally the most radical. In fact, one may justifiably accuse the cable news network of suffering collective Obama Derangement Syndrome. Others call it the birth of white minority politics. But the Christian Right's obsession with Obama has become so widespread that more than 50 percent of Republicans surveyed in August 2010 thought it was "definitely true" that Obama "sympathizes with the goals of fundamentalists who want to impose Islamic law around the world." It's now 2013, and still more than 25 percent of Republicans believe Obama was born outside of the United States, even despite the fact that the President did what no other previous president was asked to do, presented his birth certificate to the U.S. public. The Right's over-the-top hatred for a sitting U.S. president is unparalleled in recent times, possibly ever. The day after Obama was sworn in as president, Rush Limbaugh said, "I hope he fails!" Those four words may seem innocuous enough, but consider the fact that at the time the Limbaugh muttered those words, the country was fighting two wars, while dealing with an economy that was losing 800,000 jobs per month. Again, further proof that if their ideological appointees are not at the helm, the Christian Right holds little affection for America. The leader of the Republican Party in the Senate, Mitch McConnell, said his number one priority was "to ensure Obama becomes a one term president." He never did say how far down his list creating jobs for the middle class was. The attacks on the Fox News network were worse. Sarah Palin said to Sean Hannity on his show, "Obama's philosophy of radicalism is a throwback to the days before the Civil War, and he's moving the country backwards to those days when we were in different classes based on income, based on color of skin." Glenn Beck went one step further, if that were at all possible, in telling his viewers, "Obama has a deep-seated hatred for white people."

All in all, this whipped-up hysteria against Obama has left the economy in a ditch with no real economic recovery in sight, and even when it does eventually come, it will be far too late for far too many. With the Republicans controlling the House, and with many of its representatives sent to Washington on the back of constituents suffering Fox News-induced Obama Derangement Syndrome, the economy stays stuck in second gear, because seemingly the GOP has only two mandates: block Obama, even if it means trashing the economy to achieve that objective; and tax cuts for the wealthy. Michael Cohen, columnist at the *Guardian*, wrote:

> Republicans have opposed a lion's share of stimulus measures that once they supported, such as a payroll tax break, which they grudgingly embraced earlier this year. Even unemployment insurance, a relatively uncontroversial tool for helping those in an economic downturn, has been consistently held up by Republicans or used as a bargaining chip for

more tax cuts. Ten years ago, prominent conservatives were loudly making the case for fiscal stimulus to get the economy going; today, they treat such ideas like they're the plague.

Traditionally, during economic recessions, Republicans have been supportive of loose monetary policy. Not this time. Rather, Republicans have upbraided Ben Bernanke, head of the Federal Reserve, for even considering policies that focus on growing the economy and creating jobs. And then, there is the fact that since the original stimulus bill passed in February of 2009, Republicans have made practically no effort to draft comprehensive job creation legislation. Instead, they continue to pursue austerity policies, which reams of historical data suggest harms economic recovery and does little to create jobs. In fact, since taking control of the House of Representatives in 2011, Republicans have proposed hardly a single major jobs bill that didn't revolve, in some way, around their one-stop solution for all the nation's economic problems: more tax cuts.

In Obama's first term, the GOP objective was to make Obama a one-term president. In his second, it's to trash the economy so bad that his legacy will be ruined forever. Effectively, they want his presidency to be little more than an asterisk in the pages of history. That's how much these crazies on the right hate America. That's how much they hate democracy. For them there's only solution for this country, a theocratic regime sponsored by WalMart.

Sadly, the mainstream media is so insipid and gutless that the Republican Party can get away with whatever devious and unpatriotic tactic serves their ideological purposes, even if it means intentionally trashing the economy, which it is clear they are doing. Robert Reich believes the GOP controlled congress is intentionally keeping unemployment high to keep their corporate sponsors happy, for high unemployment keeps wages down; low wages help boost corporate profits; high unemployment fuels company stock prices on Wall Street, which keeps the Fed committed to buying long-term bonds. Also, high unemployment keeps Americans economically fearful and financially insecure, which sets them up to believe the myriad regressive economic lies the Republican Party tells in attacking Obama, i.e. that big government will take away the little their base has, and give it to the "undeserving moochers" (read minorities), thus they should support tax cuts for corporations and the wealthy "job creators".

A functioning media would expose the Right's manipulation of the public and the economic mistruths it makes, but the fourth estate is no longer performing its role.

In a review of McChesney and Nichols' *Death and Life of American Journalism,* Chris Hedges writes:

> As utopian fantasies go, this is pretty good. But it ignores the critical shift within American society from a print-based culture to an image-based culture. It assumes, incorrectly, that people still value and want traditional news. They do not. We have become unmoored from a world of print, from complexity and nuance, and with it information systems built on the primacy of verifiable fact. Newspapers, which engage rather than entertain, can no longer compete with the emotional battles that hyperventilating hosts on trash talk shows mount daily. The public, which has walked away

from newspapers, has embraced the emotional carnival that has turned news into another form of mindless entertainment.

A thriving democracy is dependent upon a well-educated electorate. When you combine the death of journalism in this country with the resurgence of the bible-thumping mouth-breathers of the South, we are a long way from realizing a thriving democracy.

CHAPTER FIFTEEN
THE POLICE SURVEILLANCE STATE

"None are more hopelessly enslaved than those who falsely believe they are free."

JOHANN WOLFGANG VON GOETHE

On the evening of July 4, 2012, a SWAT team of 12 officers assembled 50 yards from the driveway of Matthew David Stewart's home. With night-vision goggles, flak jackets, balaclavas and helmets, the 'platoon' did a final weapons check before moving towards their target. Their weapons included some of the most sophisticated military assault machine guns the battlefield has ever seen. Inside the home, Stewart lay asleep. His crime? The SWAT team was acting on a tip from Stewart's former girlfriend, who had contacted the police claiming the accused was growing marijuana in his basement.

Stewart was a U.S. military veteran with no prior criminal record. With no announcement, and without identifying themselves as police officers, the commando-attired intruders kicked his front door down and burst suddenly into his living room. Stewart was awoken. Thinking criminals were invading his home, as he later described, he grabbed his 9-millimeter pistol, and began shooting wildly towards his assailants. In the chaos and confusion, the police fired more than 250 rounds, hitting and wounding Stewart twice. Stewart fired 31 rounds, wounding six officers, and killing one.

In the aftermath, no evidence was found whatsoever that the 16 small marijuana plants in Stewart's basement were grown for the purpose of selling. None. In fact, Stewart had been diagnosed with PTSD after serving a tour in Iraq, and had smoked marijuana to self-medicate.

Stewart was charged with the murder of Officer Jared Francom. After failing to contest the legitimacy of the search warrant, he hung himself alone in his prison cell.

Welcome to one of the most disturbing trends in American policing: the militarization of police weaponry and tactics. The para-militirization of police departments across the country is leading to a police force that sees itself at war with the American people. And guess whom we have to blame for that? Correct, our friends on the Christian Right. Again!

Christianity's simplistic worldview divides the world into two halves: sinners versus do-gooders. Evil versus righteousness. Christian versus infidel. Good versus bad. Black versus white. In their narrow minds, there is no grey; there is no nuance. As George W. Bush said, "You're either with us or against us." With this Bronze Age mindset, the Christian Right has embraced crime as an essential test for government. They push the Republican Party to spend more and more on aggressive policing tactics and outrageous budgets. Of course, this serves the GOP's corporate masters well, too, as the ultimate beneficiaries of these policies are the weapons and defense manufacturers. Ian Lopez, author of *After the War on Crime*, writes, "From a big-picture point of view, the welfare state is fighting the warfare state. The old-style liberals, the old Democratic Party is fighting desperately somehow to defend the old welfare state, the Great Society, the New Deal, all the achievements of the last century, and they are losing. They are losing out to this right-wing vision of a warfare state that the government shouldn't be in the business of helping people, but it should be in the business of keeping order domestically and globally. This vision of a leaner, meaner, primarily violent state – this is the debate as we find it: the nanny state versus the Robocop state."

The police attack on Stewart was no anomaly. The proliferation of SWAT teams across America has been extreme. Police departments in the smallest of localities now have massive firepower: helicopters, drones, tanks, bayonets, and explosives. Yes, bayonets! In case you don't know what exactly a SWAT team is, SWAT is an acronym for Special Weapons And Tactics. They're special police units that use military-style light weapons and specialized tactics in high-risk operations that generally fall outside the capabilities of regular, uniformed police. That was their initially intended purpose. Today, however, they're using their battering rams, incendiary devices, and flashbang grenades to overpower low-level, non-violent pot dealers and/or their users.

The growth and use of these paramilitary police forces has been parabolic. For example, consider that in 1980 there were 3,000 SWAT raids conducted. In 2012, there were 50,000 SWAT raids. That's a 1500 percent increase in 30 years. Also, consider the fact that a majority of those raids were conducted on non-violent, consensual drug crimes.

Radly Balko, who wrote *Rise of the Warrior Cop*, writes:

> Since the 1960s, in response to a range of perceived threats, law-enforcement agencies across the U.S., at every level of government, have been blurring the line between police officer and soldier. Driven

by martial rhetoric and the availability of military-style equipment—from bayonets and M-16 rifles to armored personnel carriers—American police forces have often adopted a mind-set previously reserved for the battlefield. The war on drugs and, more recently, post-9/11 antiterrorism efforts have created a new figure on the U.S. scene: the warrior cop—armed to the teeth, ready to deal harshly with targeted wrongdoers, and a growing threat to familiar American liberties.

According to surveys conducted by the criminologist Peter Kraska of Eastern Kentucky University, just 13 percent of towns with populations of between 25,000 and 50,000 people had a SWAT team in 1983. By 2005, the figure was up to 80 percent. Cities are using federal grants to scale up all kinds of weaponry, including procurement of armored vehicles, like that of the Lenco BearCat, which is really a monstrous military tank, to be deployed on the streets of America. According to the Center for Investigative Reporting, the Department of Homeland Security has doled out more than $35 billion in grants since its creation in 2002, with much of the money going to purchase military gear such as armored personnel carriers. In 2011 alone, a Pentagon program for bolstering the capabilities of local law enforcement gave away $500 million of equipment, an all-time high.

Right there is the kicker. The DHS is effectively incentivizing police departments to arrest low-level, non-violent pot dealers. For every pot-related arrest a police department makes, they are awarded cash in the form of annual federal grants. These grants are then used to procure more and more weaponry and all the toys that allow cops to dress up like they were walking the streets of Fallujah. But there's no such federal funding for catching murderers, rapists, pedophiles, kidnappers, and other violent offenders. Think about this: if you were a cop, would you risk harm to yourself by walking into the house of a known violent offender, or would you burst into a college dorm to arrest a guy who passes on a few joints of weed to his pals? And if you were that city's police commissioner, what would you have your cops focus on? It's obvious this policy is causing our police departments to misplace priorities and, in doing so, they're making our communities less safe.

In August 2013, Attorney General Eric Holder made the two giant steps forward towards implementing more sensible drug laws. First he announced the Justice Department would move to end mandatory minimum sentences for drug possession charges. Second he announced the federal government would allow Washington and Colorado to move forward and implement new state laws legalizing recreational marijuana use by adults. Finally, some common fucking sense, right? Given the only entities that profit from legalized drugs are the cartels, cops and the private prisons, a predictable response in the form of a letter was sent to Holder on behalf of a broad coalition of law enforcement officers, sheriffs, and big city police chiefs – who have spent the past three decades waging an increasingly militarized and failed war. In summary, the letter expressed "extreme disappointment" in the Justice Department's decision. "The decision will undoubtedly have grave unintended consequences, including a reversal of the declining crime rates that we as law enforcement practitioners have spent more than a decade maintaining." What the letter did not mention is the fact that the war on drugs has not reduced pot's popularity, or the fact that our prison population has tripled thanks to incarcerating people for smoking a plant. By decriminalizing pot, states are able to tax it, and then use that money to fight the real drug-related plagues of the country – like poverty. But police departments aren't concerned about that, they are concerned about the loss of funding. In other words, the revenue they lose by seizing assets during drug raids, and the grants they get for making drug user arrests.

This all harks back to when President Nixon launched the War on Drugs when he said in 1971, "America's public enemy number one is drug abuse." Now think about that. In Nixon's eyes, a person doing drugs in the privacy of their own home is more of a threat to Americans than violent offenders. Thus commencing a backwards mindset on the way Americans viewed crime and the drug problem. Moreover, it indoctrinated our police with a military mindset. We tell officers they're fighting a war, and then we encourage them to dress like soldiers. It's a them versus us mentality. One that sees all citizens as potential enemies, and innocents caught in the crossfire as collateral damage. Heck, the testosterone-filled military rhetoric has made its way from the beat cop all the way to executive office. New York Mayor Michael Bloomberg once boasted, "In the NYPD, I have the 7th largest army in the world."

Van Jones wrote:

> We have a problem about understanding what this radicalized policing and radicalized oppression is. It's so awful that it is hard to look at. One of the things going on is that there has been a shotgun wedding between the prison-industrial complex

and the military-industrial complex. The war on crime is really a series of wars; the war on drugs, which is really war on black people, and the war on terror, which is a war on immigrants, Arabs, and Muslims; and it's that far-fetched. These two wars are basically the same thing; they re fought against a faceless radicalized enemy that's both at home and abroad. An open-ended war gets declared, and there's no particular strategy to resolve it except policify and take away rights, and there's no end-game. That's the war on drugs. It's the war on terror. So what we face now is the prospect of a seam-less web of repression, from Oakland to Baghdad, with the U.S. government being violent inside the U.S. border, violent at the U.S. border, and violent beyond the U.S. border. We are facing a national surveillance security state.

According to John W. Whitehead – founder of the Ruther-ford Institute, a non-profit civil liberties and human rights organization – more Americans may find themselves in in-creasingly dangerous situations as SWAT teams are used more frequently in routine law enforcement activities.

The rapid growth of battlefield-styled police forces is even more remarkable when you consider the steady de-cline of violent crime since the 1990s. Sociologists are not sure exactly why violent crime has fallen so precipitously, but the fact is, it has! Thus, it's only reasonable to ask why is America becoming ever increasingly a paramilitarized police and surveillance state. If you consider that politi-cians are now effectively in the business of protecting the interests of their corporate paymasters, then you many want to consider what a U.S. Marine Colonel by the name of Peter Martino recently remarked: "The U.S. government is spying on Americans because they fear Americans."

The Occupy Movement had the potential to be the most important civil disobedience of our time. People of all walks came together in cities across America to protest the social injustices that are tearing away at the fabric of society. Old, young, white, black, Latino, Asians, lawyers, street sweepers, doctors, war veterans, students, school teachers, and the rest of us joined to protest the inequality between the top 1 percent income earners and the bottom 99 percent (us). For many Americans, it was the first time they had ever taken part in a civic protest. The right to protest is one of the fundamentals that make the American experiment with democracy so great. Protests ushered in the Civil Rights Act and ended the war in Vietnam. The Occupy protests spoke to everything that is wrong with our economy and society today: that too much wealth is accumulated at the very top, which has led to injustices committed in the boardrooms, the courtrooms, the classrooms and the streets.

Enter the new police state. Enter the warrior cop.

The Department of Homeland Security, the FBI, the mayors of 18 cities, and state and local police forces all coordinated with one another to crack down on, and break up, Occupy protests across the country. Jill Klausen, who manages a political consulting firm, wrote about what she witnessed.

When we tried—peacefully—to exercise our constitutional right to assemble, we were harassed, tear-gassed, assaulted with bean bag guns and other weapons, arrested, and charged with crimes. Two innocent civilians, both Iraq War veterans, one of whom wasn't even a participant, nearly *died* as a direct result of the police brutality waged against citizens legally rallying for the attention of our government. And most of the country sat back and watched, either with indifference, or with glee. And Republicans universally supported these tyrannical government actions — cheered them on, in fact. They came at us with guns, *tasers*, batons, flash-bang devices, rubber bullets, tear gas and other chemical weapons, wearing full body armor and sporting shields to protect *themselves* from … bottles of water, maybe some rocks, and possibly a little paint.

In 2013, the U.S. district court in San Francisco awarded a group of 12 protestors one million dollars after they sued the Oakland Police Department for police brutality. One of the plaintiffs described what the Department did to her: "I was in the middle of telling OPD I loved them when they threw explosives at me. The loud explosion caused permanent hearing loss and unrelenting ringing in my ears. As a result, I can only sleep two hours at a time which has had a serious impact on my life, including adversely impacting my graduate school studies, when I graduate, and when I will be ordained. It is my hope that there will never be cause for this type of lawsuit again, and the city can instead focus its resources on supporting the marginalized and those most in need of resources, which is what we were protesting for."

Practically all Occupy protestors across all the major cities experienced police harassment of some sort. Students at the University of California, Davis, who were sitting peacefully, were pepper-sprayed directly in the face by needlessly aggressive campus police wearing riot gear and flak jackets. Yes, I did say "campus police"! In short, the way the Occupy movement was silenced by battlefield-armed police was a disgrace. The movement was, by and large, a peaceful movement. The movement was American citizens exercising their constitutional rights. If Americans are not free to exercise that right, then freedom in this country becomes hollow in meaning.

AFTERWORD

Thanks to the Supreme Court's decision to rule in favor of Citizens United, the U.S. now has a campaign finance system where an infinitesimally small slice of the American people account for than a quarter of all individual political campaign contributions. In fact, in 2012, just a tick over 31,000 individuals accounted for 25 percent of the total $6 billion in contributions from identifiable sources. 31,000 campaign contributors represent a mere one in ten thousand Americans. The 1 percent of the 1 percent are now the gatekeepers of political office in this country. In fact, every single member of Congress elected in the 2012 races received a contribution from this tiny slice of the electorate.

According to the web magazine *OpenSecrets*, nearly 90 percent of those elected received more from the "1 percent of the 1 percent" than they did from small donors. (Small donors defined as donating less than $200).

With Republican candidates receiving contributions from the richest 31,000 Americans on a scale of 2:1 over Democratic candidates, run this new dynamic to its natural conclusion: that elected officials are becoming increasingly beholden to their corporate and mega rich paymasters.

Ultimately, this is making the marriage between the Christian Right and their corporate sponsors pose an ever growing threat to not only our secular sensibilities, but also our sense of what makes America great: ideas like justice and liberty for all, free speech, separation of Church and State, and protected constitutional rights.

Thanks to the Christian Right's enthusiasm at the polls, corporations are destroying every major public accomplishment this nation has achieved. While corporations and billionaires grant the Jesus freaks the right to play out their religiously inspired social policies, Wall Street and the Koch Brothers are successfully privatizing every public welfare initiative so that they can profit from us from the moment we are born to the moment someone reads our eulogy.

A society is typically defined as a set of mutual benefits and duties that is visible by its public institutions. Often we grade societies, civilizations, and cities by their public hospitals, public schools, public transportation, public libraries, public recreation and parks, public universities, public museums, and so on. In fact, according to the Global Happiness Index, the happiest cities and countries are those with boastable public infrastructures. Countries like those of Northern Europe, Australia, and Canada. Robert Reich says,

> Public institutions are supported by all taxpayers, and are available to all. If the tax system is progressive, those who are better off (and who, presumably, have benefited from many of those same public institutions) help pay for everyone else. Whereas to "privatize" means the rest of us (individuals) must pay for it ourselves. Much of what was once public is now increasingly become owned by corporations, which means ever-higher tolls on public highways, higher college tuition costs, and higher admission fees at once public parks and museums. If the rich get their way to privatize Social Security, banks will finally be able to gouge your retirement funds with inexplicable fees and costs.

Corporations are on the way to creating a new "two Americas". Under the old paradigm, the two Americas were defined as liberals versus conservatives. Under the new, it will be rich versus poor, with no middle class. For those who are rich enough to afford private education, the best private hospitals and to live behind gate-guarded communities with manicured lawns, pools, and security contractors, they will enjoy the rich America. For those at the economic bottom, they will be left with public infrastructure that is shoddy and decrepit; with deteriorated and under resourced schools; cities with a lack of police; and hospitals with battlefield-like emergency rooms. But not to worry, the poor America will still have an abundance of churches to ensure the poor don't rise up and murder the rich, and they will also enjoy the "comforts" of the nation's for-profit prisons, for they will never able to able to afford for-profit universities.

Corporations are getting away with redesigning America in their own image because the Christian Right is so enthusiastically voting for the business party. That's where social wedge politics and culture wars come in. Pushing an agenda to destroy Social Security doesn't get a lot of evangelicals excited to vote, but on the other hand, laws prohibiting abortion and sodomy does.

The culture war allows the Christian Right and the Tea Party to sustain the delusion that is speaks for the majority. By wrapping AR15 Bushmaster automatic weapons and the crucifix in American flags, the religious lunatics derive power from falsely believing they represent the "real America". Their shill and high-pitch proclamations about "taking America back" and "restoring traditional values" tend to resound above our rational discourse. As a result, we, the majority, tend to limit ourselves. We begin to believe that we, secularists, represent a minority in the country. We don't! As stated throughout the book, any number of polls demonstrate a majority of Americans lean left on practically all social and economic issues. Unfortunately, we tend to shrink from the ideologically driven battles, and never more so than at the polling booths, particularly at the state and local level. Also, atheists tend to limit themselves to fighting fires that have little or no consequence in the broader sense of the nation's body politick. Filing a law suit against a city that prevents it from displaying "Merry Christmas" is of far less value than ensuring corporate stooges dressed as fundamentalist Christians, like Scott Walker, Nikki Haley, and Rick Perry, are prevented from gaining office, so that they cannot enact the corporate-driven religiously conservative agenda.

It's demographic fact that angry, white Christians are becoming a smaller slice of the electorate, but we can't rely on demographics to win these battles for us. The year 2050 is still a way off. For now, extreme right-wing fruitcakes are a smaller piece of the American pie – and yet they are winning. Nay, they are routing the board.

I hope the atheist community, which is now sizeable and organized, becomes a potent political movement. A movement that not only has the potential to match the Christian Right in terms of organization, but also in terms of political agitation. For the atheist movement to remain apolitical is no longer an option. To stay the course will mean we continue to win the small battles, like removing mention of God from the currency, while continuing to lose the broader war.

There are many ways the atheist movement can harness its ever-growing electoral mass and be as equally or more politically influential than the Republican base – the Christian Right. In their book *It's Even Worse Than it Looks*, Mann and Ornstein prescribe reforms for improving the performance of America's dysfunctional politics, reforms that would put an end to the radical far Right driving the Republican Party's agenda. One such recommended reform is to make voting mandatory, like it is in Australia and thirty-one other nations:

> Higher turnout would pull more citizens with less-fixed partisan and ideological commitments into the electorates. Near universal voting would virtually eliminate the parties' incentive to diminish the turnout of those likely to support their opponent and to mobilize their strongest supporters....In both primaries and general elections in the United States, party professionals and consultants focus on bases: how to gin up the turnout of the party's ideological base and suppress the turnout of the other side....It has encouraged a concentration of hot-button issues that appeal to the party bases, like guns, abortion, immigration, and same-sex marriage, and led to more and more extreme rhetoric and exaggerated positions to accomplish the larger political goals.

The Congress could pass a law making poll attendance mandatory for federal primary and general elections, but that is unlikely anytime soon given that surveys show a substantial majority of Americans oppose the idea of compulsory voting. But if atheists and/or progressives make this one of their primary political goals, with the objective to diminish the corporate driven theocratic threat, then the secularist community could play a major role in educating the public on the benefits that expanding the vote would have for the political system.

The moment for the atheist movement to organize, mobilize, and evangelize politically is now. Otherwise, The Theocratic Republic of the Corporate United States of America will increasingly become our reality. So, what are you going to do about it?

REFERENCES

Chuck Thompson, *Better Off Without Em': A Northern Manifesto for Southern Secession* (Simon & Schuster 2012)

Michael Lind, "The South versus Obama":
http://www.thedailybeast.com/articles/2009/01/29/the-south-rises-again.html

University of Rochester: "The Political Legacy of Slavery":
http://www.mattblackwell.org/files/papers/slavery.pdf

ARIS 2008: "American Religious Identification Survey":
http://commons.trincoll.edu/aris/

Putman & Campbell, *American Grace: How Religion Divides and Unites Us* (Simon & Schuster 2010)

Jonathan Alter, *The Center Holds* (Simon & Schuster 2013)

Robert Reich, "Why Republicans Want Jobs to Stay Anemic":
http://www.huffingtonpost.com/robert-reich/obama-jobs-republicans_b_3703612.html

Paul Krugman, *The Great Unraveling: Losing our Way in the New Century* (W.M & Norton 2003)

Paul Krugman *New York Times* op-ed articles:
http://krugman.blogs.nytimes.com/

BLS: "Job growth under Presidents":

http://www.cleveland.com/datacentral/index.ssf/2010/10/us_job_growth_and_loss_under_p.html

Herman Schwartz, "Democrats, it's the States, Stupid":
http://blogs.reuters.com/great-debate/2013/07/14/democrats-its-the-states-stupid/

Katrina vanden Heuvel, "The GOP's state-by-state crusade to disenfranchise voters": http://articles.washingtonpost.com/2011-

07-26/opinions/35237134_1_voter-fraud-voter-impersonation-disenfranchise

Michael Waldman, Brennan Center for Justice, "Voting Rights Act": http://www.brennancenter.org/video/msnbc-michael-waldman-voting-rights-act

Alexander Keyssar, *The Right To Vote* (Basic Books 2009)

Cass R. Sunstein, *Radicals in Robes: Why Extreme Right Wing Courts Are Wrong for America* (Basic Books 2006)

Mark Moulitsas, *American Taliban* (Polipoint Press 2010)

University of Connecticut, "Declining Public Concern About Climate Change" http://sp.uconn.edu/~scruggs/gec11.pdf

James Fallows, "SCOTUS Update: La Loi, Cest Moi" : http://www.theatlantic.com/politics/archive/2012/06/scotus-update-la-loi-cest-moi/258900/

Cornwall Alliance for the Stewardship of Creation, *Resisting the Green Dragon*. (2011)

Yale Project on Climate Change Communication: http://environment.yale.edu/climate-communication/

Jeff Sharlett, *The Family* (Harper Collins 2009).

Charles Wilson and William R. Ferris, *The Encyclopedia of Southern Culture* (University of North Carolina Press 1989)

Barna Group Study: "Diversity of Faith in Various Cities": https://www.barna.org/barna-update/faith-spirituality/435-diversity-of-faith-in-various-us-cities

Center for Economic Policy and Research: "Why the Minimum Wage has no Discernable Effect on Employment": http://www.cepr.net/documents/publications/min-wage-2013-02.pdf

James Surowiecki, "The Pay is Too Damn Low":
http://www.newyorker.com/talk/financial/2013/08/12/1308
12ta_talk_surowiecki

Virginia Commonwealth University (2006): "Estimating State IQ":
http://www.people.vcu.edu/~mamcdani/Publications/McDanie
l%20(2006)%20Estimating%20state%20IQ.pdf

Thomas Franks, *Pity the Billionaire* (Picador 2012)

Terry O'Neill, "The Romney-Ryan Budget: Who Are the Real
Moochers in their Medicaid Scheme?":
http://www.huffingtonpost.com/terry-oneill/medicaid-
romney-ryan_b_1911113.html

David K. Shipler, *The Working Poor: Invisible in America* (First
Vintage Books 2005)

Citizens for Tax Justice: "Tax Payers and Tax Dodgers 2008-2010":
http://www.ctj.org/corporatetaxdodgers/CorporateTaxDodgers
Report.pdf

Steven Pinker, *The Better Angels of our Nature* (Penguin Group 2011)

Guttmacher Institute, "An Overview of Abortion Laws (2013)":
http://www.guttmacher.org/statecenter/spibs/spib_OAL.pdf

Chris Mooney, *Unscientific America* (Basic Books 2009)

Chris Hedges, *American Fascists* (Free Press 2008)

David Blair and Jay Barth, *Arkansas Politics and Government*
(University of Nebraska 2005)

John Mearsheimer and Stephen Walt, *The Israeli Lobby and U.S.
Foreign Policy* (Farrar, Straus, and Girox 2007)

Martin Lee, *Unreliable Sources* (LGLA 2013)

Kathleen Jamieson, *Echo Chamber: Rush Limbaugh and the
Conservative Media Establishment* (Oxford University Press 2008)

Eric Alterman, *What Liberal Media?* (Basic Books 2008)

Ian Lopez, Mary Frampton, Jonathan Simon,*After the War on Crime* (NYU Press 2008)

Radley Balko, *Rise of the Warrior Cop: The Militarization of America's Police Forces* (Public Affairs 2013)

Thomas E. Mann and Norman J. Ornstein, *It's Even Worse Than It Looks* (Basic Books 2012)

Robert McChesney and John Nichols, *The Death and Life of American Journalism* (Nation Books 2011)

Susan Jacoby, *The Age of American Unreason* (Vintage Press 2009)

Neil Postman, *Entertaining Ourselves to Death* (Penguin Books 2005)

Robert Reich, "The Myth of the Free Market and How to Make the Economy Work for Us": http://www.huffingtonpost.com/robert-reich/free-market_b_3935173.html

Drew Westin, *The Political Brain: The Role of the Emotion in Deciding the Fate of the Nation* (Public Affairs 2008)

Union Membership Rates in 24 Countries: http://www.bls.gov/opub/mlr/2006/01/art3full.pdf

Katherine O'Brien & Rourke O'Brien, *Taxing the Poor* (University of California Press 2011)

Mayer, Jane. "State for Sale." The New Yorker, October 10, 2011. http://www.newyorker.com/reporting/2011/10/10/111010fa_fact_mayer.

Carter, Dan. "North Carolina: A State of Shock": http://southernspaces.org/2013/north-carolina-state-shock

Michael Grunwald, *The New New Deal.* (Simon & Schuster 2012)